WHO IS FOR PEACE?

WHO IS FOR PEACE?

BY

FRANCIS SCHAEFFER
VLADIMIR BUKOVSKY
JAMES HITCHCOCK

Thomas Nelson Publishers
Nashville • Camden • New York

Second printing, 1983

Copyright © 1983 Francis A. Schaeffer, Vladimir Bukovsky, James Hitchcock

"The Secular Humanist World View Versus the Christian World View and Biblical Perspectives on Military Preparedness" by Francis A. Schaeffer, copyright © 1983.

"The Peace Movement and the Soviet Union" by Vladimir Bukovsky, copyright © 1982.

"The Catholic Bishops' Search for Peace" by James Hitchcock, copyright © 1983.

Published in Nashville, Tennessee, by Thomas Nelson, Inc. and distributed in Canada by Lawson Falle, Ltd., Cambridge, Ontario.

Printed in the United States of America.

Library of Congress Cataloging in Publication Data

Schaeffer, Francis A. (Francis August)
 Who is for peace?

 Includes bibliographical references.
 Contents: The secular humanist world view versus the
Christian world view and Biblical perspectives on military preparedness / by Francis A. Schaeffer—The
Peace Movement and the Soviet Union / by Vladimir
Bukovsky—The Catholic bishops' search for peace /
by James Hitchcock.
 1. War—Religious aspects—Christianity—Addresses,
essays, lectures. 2. Peace (Theology)—Addresses, essays,
lectures. 3. National security—Religious aspects—
Christianity—Addresses, essays, lectures. 4. Secular-
ism—Controversial literature—Addresses, essays,
lectures. 5. Humanism—Controversial literature—
Addresses, essays, lectures. 6. Soviet Union—Military
policy—Addresses, essays, lectures. 7. Atomic
warfare—Religious aspects—Catholic Church—Addresses,
essays, lectures. 8. Catholic Church—Doctrines—
Addresses, essays, lectures. I. Bukovskiĭ, Vladimir
Konstantinovich, 1942-   . II. Hitchcock, James.
III. Title.
BT736.2.S3   1983   261.8'73   83-17482
ISBN 0-8407-5878-2

Contents

Introduction

Francis Schaeffer, Vladimir Bukovsky, and James Hitchcock are, at first glance, an unlikely group of authors to collaborate on a book. But there is something that ties them together: a basic realism and common sense concerning the dilemma of war and peace, particularly the nuclear arms question.

In theologian Francis Schaeffer, evangelical Protestant Christianity finds its spokesman. In historian James Hitchcock, traditional Roman Catholicism has an able defender. In writer Vladimir Bukovsky, the world has been given not only a man of extraordinary personal bravery but, as a Soviet dissident who has now lived in the West for seven years, a rare opportunity to see the world through the eyes of one who has lived within the Soviet Union *and* the United States. He has seen the nuclear arms question from both sides of the fence.

What these three writers have in common is that they distrust the facile and simplistic utopian solutions being presented by the "peace" movement today concerning how to attain world peace through nuclear "disarmament."

Their adversaries in the peace movement come from a

7

long line of isolationists and pacificists in the United States and other Western countries. The only other time in recent history that this isolationism and pacificism became part of a large national consensus was the period between the First and Second World Wars in Great Britain. From that era of history we learn that those who espouse "peace at any price" often are the ones who, in the end, open the way for national, and even global, tragedy through war. The policy of appeasement and pacificism, pursued by politicians such as Stanley Baldwin and Neville Chamberlain in the face of the Nazi German threat in the 1930s, is being promoted today by the peace movement regarding the USSR.

In the 1930s the voice of Winston Churchill rang out clearly, even during what has been known as Churchill's "wilderness years," when he was out of office and few people were heeding his warnings. Nevertheless, he did not give up speaking the truth. Similarly, Francis Schaeffer, Vladimir Bukovsky, and James Hitchcock are lonely voices trying to remind people that planet Earth is, after all, a globe peopled by sinful individuals and that, even if well intentioned, *utopian simplistic solutions to the problem of war may generate the opposite of the intended results.* Indeed, then, this book is appropriately entitled *Who Is for Peace?*

Alexander Solzhenitsyn was quoted in a *Wall Street Journal* interview on June 23, 1983, as saying,

> It is normal to be afraid of nuclear weapons. I would condemn no one for that. But the generation now coming out of Western schools is unable to distinguish good from bad. Even those words are unacceptable. This results in impaired thinking ability. . . . These young people will soon look back on photographs of their own demonstrations and cry. But it will be too late. I say to them: You are protesting

nuclear arms, but are you prepared to defend your homeland with non-nuclear arms? No. These people are unprepared for *any* kind of struggle.

Solzhenitsyn here goes to the heart of the matter: Western democracies, under the influence of relativistic, secular thinking, particularly secular humanistic philosophy, seem to have lost a coherent belief system that enables them to fight for anything, either with words or arms.

Often the debate about nuclear weapons rages on as if that were the only issue in regard to war, but beneath the surface there is a more profound debate, one that poses the question, Is there anything in life worth fighting for? Or for that matter even worth struggling for intellectually?

In these times of wavering indifference, it is refreshing to read the essays in this book. The authors are not indifferent towards such ideas as absolute truth, right and wrong, good and evil. And they have been willing to lay aside their differences of religious belief to issue a warning to those who would make hasty decisions in regard to nuclear arms. That an orthodox Roman Catholic, an evangelical Protestant, and a well-known Soviet dissident can band together to write such a book is a testament to the seriousness with which they take their cause.

FRANKY SCHAEFFER V
August 1983

The Secular Humanist World View Versus the Christian World View
and
Biblical Perspectives on Military Preparedness

by Francis A. Schaeffer

Who Is For Peace?

This essay is based upon a lecture given at the Mayflower Hotel in Washington, D.C., on May 22, 1982. The host committee for the Washington meeting were:

The Honorable and Mrs. James G. Watt
The Honorable and Mrs. James B. Edwards
The Honorable and Mrs. Terrel H. Bell
The Honorable and Mrs. Edwin Meese, III
The Honorable and Mrs. Strom Thurmond
The Honorable Jennings Randolph
The Honorable and Mrs. Howard H. Baker, Jr.
The Honorable and Mrs. Jeremiah A. Denton, Jr.
The Honorable William V. Alexander
The Honorable and Mrs. Jack F. Kemp
The Honorable and Mrs. Carlos J. Moorhead
The Honorable and Mrs. J. Marvin Leath
The Honorable and Mrs. C. William Nelson
The Honorable and Mrs. Charles W. Stenholm
The Honorable and Mrs. James L. Buckley
General and Mrs. John William Vessey, Jr.
Mrs. Mary C. Crowley
Mr. Larry Lightner
Mr. James E. Lyon
Mr. and Mrs. Robert L. Parker
Mr. and Mrs. Robert M. Pittenger
Mr. and Mrs. George F. Will

FRANCIS A. SCHAEFFER *founded L'Abri Fellowship, an international study center and community in Switzerland with branches in England, The Netherlands, Sweden, and the United States. Among his most influential books are* The God Who is There, Escape From Reason, He Is There and He Is Not Silent, *and* The Mark of the Christian. *Dr. Schaeffer has lectured frequently at leading universities in the United States and abroad, and his books have been translated into twenty-five languages.*

The theme of this essay may at first appear to be a double one, but actually the two halves are not in conflict: as we shall see, they make one unity.

First of all, we must be very careful to define what we mean by humanism. We are not talking about humanitarianism, being kind to people. As Christians, of course, we should be more humanitarian than anyone else. We must be equally careful not to confuse humanism and the Humanities, which refers to the study of human creativity. These studies include "classical" learning, but they extend to the whole field of human creativity. Christians above everyone should be interested in the Humanities. Many of my own books, films, articles, and speeches deal with a Christian consideration and love of the Humanities. This topic is crucial because Christianity views human creativity as an essential mark of our having been made in the image of God.

What, then, is humanism? The term *humanism* means Man beginning from himself, with no knowledge except what he himself can discover and no standard outside of himself. In this view Man is the measure of all things, as the Enlightenment expressed it. In other words, mankind can only look to itself for solutions to its problems and never looks to God either for salvation or for moral direction. Humanism can be seen, then, as the ultimate attempt to pull one's self up by one's own bootstraps.

One thing must be clear at the outset: there can be no concord between humanism and the Christian world view. We must realize that the contrast goes back to two different views of final reality.

What is final reality? In the Judeo-Christian world view, final reality is the infinite-personal God who truly is there, objectively, whether we think He is there or not. He is not there just because we think He is there. He is there objectively. And He is the Creator. He is the Creator of everything that is not Himself. We must never forget that one of the distinguishing marks of the Judeo-Christian God is that not everything is the same to Him. He has a character, and some things conform to His character and some things conflict with it. To this God (in contrast to what we find in Buddhism and Hinduism, for example) things are not neutral. Therefore, there are absolutes; there is right and wrong in the world.

But there is another view of final reality, which is being taught in our schools and which forms the framework for much of the thinking and writing of our day. In this view, final reality is thought of as purely material—or as mere energy, eventually—which has existed eternally in some form, and which has its present configuration by pure chance.

The real issue, then, is the question of final reality. The crucial point is what that final reality is: either it is to be found in the infinite-personal God, or in an impersonal and strictly material system, totally neutral to any values, lacking any interest in man as man. In this latter view, final reality yields no value system, no basis for law, and no concept of man as unique and important.

About eighty years ago in the United States we began to move from a Judeo-Christian consensus, or ethos, toward a humanist consensus. The last forty years have seen the maturing of this movement. Anyone who is fifty years old or older has witnessed the whole dramatic shift in his or her own adult lifetime. Today we must say, with tears, that the overriding consensus in our country, and in the Western world, is no longer Judeo-Christian; it has been supplanted by humanism, with its idea that final reality is only matter, eternally existing and shaped by pure chance.

There is no value system to be derived from humanism's description of final reality. No one has said it better than Jacques Monod, the French Nobel laureate in biology. In his popular book *Chance and Necessity,* he pointed out that, given this "materialistic" understanding of things, we are obliged to admit that there is no way to determine the "ought" from the "is." None at all. He himself held this view, but he saw the conclusion of it. That is, man must make himself the measure of all things; he has no alternative.

The phenomena that have arisen in our era which have troubled us are the inevitable results of this world view. If, for example, you hold this view, you must maintain that there is no source of knowledge beyond what man can find for himself. All revelation is ruled out; certainty concerning knowledge is ruled out; fixed values are ruled out. Indeed, there can be no value system at all except that which is totally arbitrary. This view leaves us with no final value system, and therefore with only personal, arbitrary, relative values. It is not only Professor Joseph Fletcher who teaches situational ethics today: the humanistic view of final reality cancels all possibility of any ethic other than the situational.

But more serious than these personal and arbitrary value systems is the fact that we are left with only an arbitrary basis for law as well. Law becomes only the decision of one person or a small group of people and what he or they decide at a given moment is for the good of society or is to their own advantage. That is because this view of final reality supplies no clue as to what law should be and the whole matter is left up to us—one man or some group, some caucus or committee, or the Supreme Court—to make the decision as to what is good for society at the moment.

Thus we end up with relative personal values and arbitrary law.

There is also the loss of any intrinsic dignity attached to the individual person. Here, significantly, lies the reason that today there is general acceptance of what would have been thought to be an abomination just a few years ago, namely abortion on demand. The practice has expanded rapidly into infanticide, that is, the killing of babies after they are born if they do not measure up to someone's notion of "life worthy to be lived." This in turn proceeds toward euthanasia, especially with respect to the aged.

This is a natural result of the materialist view of final reality and the consequent diminishing of the value of human life. An inert, impersonal final reality can have nothing to say about any real, much less unique, value attached to human life. In our own country the consequences of this view show up dramatically in the abortion-infanticide-euthanasia sequence.

When Dr. C. Everett Koop (who is now Surgeon General), my son Franky, and I produced the book and film "Whatever Happened to the Human Race?" we addressed the issue of infanticide. People thought we were fanatical, but our warnings proved all too accurate, as the Infant Doe case in Indiana illustrates. In that case a Down's Syndrome child was permitted to starve to death, with court approval, on the basis of the parents' decision not to prolong his life.

There is a headlong progression from abortion to the

terminating of small children's lives and thence to the terminating of *anyone's* life—anyone who by reason of extreme age, illness, or some other form of "nonviability" is judged to be a candidate for "positive action." (We may thank Dr. Joseph Fletcher for this felicitous synonym for the more blunt Saxon word *killing.*) The speed with which we moved from legalized abortion to the practice of infanticide suggests the connection all too starkly. Not merely the loss of an unborn baby's life or an infant's life is at stake: it is the loss of a whole view of the unique value of human life.

It is also, ironically, the loss of compassion. The irony lies in the simultaneous rise of "compassion" as a sort of banner under which all sorts of "social concern" marches, and the incredibly swift increase in the practice of abortion and infanticide. It would be a somewhat delicate task, surely, to interpret this use of the word *compassion* to the unborn babies and infants in question!

The point, of course, is that when you have jettisoned any fixed and transcendent reality that invests human life with unique and objective value, you have opened the sluiceway: you cannot shut off the surge toward a wholly valueless appraisal of human life. You cannot derive the notion of value from mere biology. What applies to the unborn applies to infants, and *a priori,* to the rest of us. There is no real reason for compassion toward people.

I plead with those of you who are in government not to allow other matters to obscure from you the critical need for taking a stand against this devaluing of human life. Many weighty matters claim your attention, but those of you who are Christians must realize the absolutely unbreakable link between the existence of the God of the Bible, who is both infinite and personal, and the unique place of human life, derived as it is from Him and made in His image.

If the uniqueness of human life continues to be compromised legally, or worse, is actually denied, we will, in fact, find not only other forms of "compassionate" killing increasing, but the ebbing away of compassion itself into cynicism.

If anyone, especially those of you in government, thinks the issue is small, I plead with you to think again. Hitherto the whole fabric of human life in the Western tradition has rested on Judeo-Christian underpinnings. These are being pulled away. Furthermore, there is a grim and elegant irony at work: the task of undermining the Judeo-Christian understanding of the uniqueness and dignity of human life is being carried forward by none other than the two ancient guardians of life, namely medicine and law. In these disciplines we see compassion being defined, more and more, in pragmatic and utilitarian terms. No taboo shelters the shrine of human life; it, along with all other phenomena, is mere data.

The First Amendment has been not only neutralized but also reversed. What began as a sanction against a state church for the thirteen states, and against the state imposing religion or interfering with the free expression of religion, is being interpreted in our own day to mean that no religious considerations should be admitted to the realm of public decision making. Religious, especially Christian, values are isolated from the governmental process.

The terror is that increasingly in the last forty years government, and especially the courts, has been the vehicle for forcing the nonreligious world view on American society. It is our government, by its laws and its court rulings, that has brought this about.

We find, as we look at our country now, that we have a largely humanistic consensus, or ethos. Ours is a humanistic culture. But happily this consensus and culture is not yet total: there is still what we might call a Christian "memory," although this is ebbing away with enormous speed.

Our calling is clear: we who hold the Christian world view, and who love human life, and who affirm humanity as bearing the image of God, should stand firm—first for the honor of God, but also for the preservation of "human*ness*."

We must, furthermore, protest the notion of manifest destiny that permits our nation to do anything it chooses. For if we insist on walking down this road, then at some point—as God is God, the God in whose eyes there is real good and real evil—we who have trampled so completely on all of God's amazing gifts to this country are going to wake up and find that He cares very much what we do. We must not suppose that we are playing only intellectual and political games. If God exists, and if He judges good and evil, then we must realize that those who trample on His great gifts will one day know His judgment. The Scriptures bear solemn witness to this. Our nation is not immune.

The first part of our topic dealt with the secular humanistic world view versus the Christian world view. I have been dealing largely with our own country. The second half concerns biblical perspectives on our nation in its international setting, in regard to military preparedness. On the surface this might appear to represent a departure from the preceding portion of this essay, but the two are not actually divergent.

When we speak of military preparedness we have very much the Soviet Union at the center of our concern. The Soviet Union, with its moorings in Marx, Engels, and Lenin, embodies the materialist world view in its most aggressive form. Marxist economic theories are not the central thing. The root of the matter is dialectical materialism. We are all familiar with the phrase. In the last analysis, the humanism which we find so energetically at work in our own country rests on the same basis, and makes the same affirmations and denials, as dialectical materialism. Final reality is merely matter, shaped by chance.

Where does it end? We may see the answer in the Marxist bloc with its radical devaluation of human life. In our own country we have seen how the humanist point of view opens the way for abortion, infanticide, and euthanasia. It is all more massive in the Communist countries because Marxism is totally committed to materialism as a world view. There are no fixed and transcendent values in that scheme. Law itself is arbitrary.

My son Franky has made a film entitled "The Second American Revolution" (Word Films, Waco, Texas). It makes a powerful statement. One of the figures in the film is Stalin, who remarks that law is simply what he himself decrees. This was Stalin's own position (we may recall the activities of the NKVD or the slaughter of the peasants in this connection, if we have some doubts on this point).

The parallel between Stalin's stark view and views which are already at work in our own country is too evident for us to miss. The difference is that, so far, these views have not been given the freedom to come to full maturity in our country whereas they have in the Marxist bloc. There we may see the inevitable conclusion of the materialist view with its corollaries of relative values and arbitrary law: the value of the individual person is lost. Only the state matters. The laws are set by an elite. There is an absoluteness about these arbitrary laws that is almost unimaginable to us in the West; yet the irony is that the elite in these "egalitarian" countries enjoy an arbitrary power that would have made Louis XIV and the czars wildly envious.

There is no objective value system. Therefore we should not be surprised that the Marxist countries which sign the Helsinki Accords then go ahead and persecute their people without a wink. Why not? The good of the state alone matters, and the good of the state is what they say it is. We in the West are naive if we imagine that we are dealing with anything other than cynicism when we enter into pacts, ententes, accords, or treaties with those who affirm the Marxist view of truth.

It is interesting that when the Soviets first came to power they passed easy abortion laws. As time went on, however, they found that this was not helpful for the state; overnight they changed these laws. Abortion then became illegal. But this turned out to be inconvenient for the state, so back they went to the easy laws. A flip-flop? No problem. Why not? All law is arbitrary.

We find, furthermore, that the low view of individual human dignity in the Marxist scheme of things takes two forms. First, we find *internal* oppression. Lenin wrote, some time before he came to power, that one of the reasons for the failure of early attempts at revolution in eighteenth-century France was that they did not kill enough people. It is fitting, on this fiftieth anniversary of the enforced starvation by Stalin of eight to ten million Ukrainians and Cossacks, to remember that this killing of their own people in the Soviet Union was a matter of state policy. And there is no difference in 1983. Solzhenitsyn, when he first left the Soviet Union, formed the Russian Social Fund to help the families of Russian dissidents imprisoned (contrary to the Soviet constitution) for reasons of conscience. He gave all the royalties from *The Gulag Archipelago* to this Swiss (and thus neutral) foundation. Soviet state policy considers it an act of treason to help such families when their means of livelihood is shut off by the imprisonment of the breadwinner of the family. In 1981 Valery Repin, who ran the Fund in Leningrad, was imprisoned until broken, then put on a show trial as a broken man. Sergei Khodorovich, the Fund's chief Soviet Union representative has also been arrested this year. Andrei Kistvakovsky has stepped into his place. Most likely he will come to the same end.[1] Christians should remember that Georgi Vins's mother, Lydia Vins, was imprisoned for three years for helping the families of imprisoned Christians. Such actions are entirely reasonable for those who devalue human life as the Soviets do. For them, oppression is not incidental to the system: it is a logical, integral, and inevitable part of their system.

Second, we find a conscious, calculated, and concerted *external* program of expansion and oppression. I beg you to understand that this is no mere fluke of one moment of Soviet history. It is an integral part of the system they hold. Just as humanism in our own country has led to abortion, infanticide, and euthanasia, so the more total expression of this same outlook, in the Soviet system, leads to both internal oppression and external expansion and oppression.

I must say, there is one point on which I admire the Soviets: since Lenin's time they have been, I think, the only country in the world with a consistent foreign policy. Unhappily for the rest of the world, this consistency has been total.

We can think back to Latvia and Estonia. Poor Latvia and Estonia. They did not want to be overrun, but they were overrun. If you visit Finland today, where people still have contacts in Latvia and Estonia, you will find sorrow because of the expansion and oppression that swallowed up those countries. There has been a constant flow of Soviet oppression, like a lava-flow, right up to the immediate history of Afghanistan and Poland. It is as natural to Soviet materialism as the abortion-infanticide-euthanasia syndrome is on our own side of the Iron Curtain.

Those of you who understand what is happening in our own country—this lowering of the worth of human life, and the giving up of fixed moral values and the transcendent base for law—ought to be able to understand what is at stake in Communist countries where materialism has been allowed to come to its full maturity, and where all the power of the absolute state guarantees the results.

Now, in the light of this natural expansion and oppression characteristic of the Soviet system, what should be our own perspective on military preparedness? Is there any light for us in the Bible?

From my own study of Scripture I would say that to refuse to do what I can for those under the power of oppressors is nothing less than a failure of Christian love. It is to refuse to love my neighbor as myself.

I do not need to appeal to a "natural law" on this point. The Bible is clear here: I am to love my neighbor as myself, in the manner needed, in a practical way, in the midst of the fallen world, at my particular point of history.

This is why I am not a pacifist. Pacifism in this poor world in which we live—this lost world—means that we desert the people who need our greatest help.

Let me illustrate: I am walking down the street and I come upon a big, burly man beating a tiny tot to death—beating this little girl—beating her—beating her. I plead with him to stop. Suppose he refuses? What does love mean now? Love means that I stop him in any way I can, including hitting him. To me this is not only necessary for humanitarian reasons: it is loyalty to Christ's commands concerning Christian love in a fallen world. What about that little girl? If I desert her to the bully, I have deserted the true meaning of Christian love—responsibility to my neighbor. She, as well as he, is my neighbor.

We have, in the Second World War, the clearest illustration anyone could ask for on this point. What about Hitler's terrorism? There was no possible way to stop the awful terror in Hitler's Germany without the use of force. There was no way.

In 1950, our family held a summer Bible school for American military dependents in Dachau. At that time the camp remained as it had been at the end of the war: it had not yet been tidied up and made into a museum. There were Polish people living nearby who had been interned, people who would have gone to the ovens within two days if the American troops had not broken down the wall with their tanks and shot their way into the camp.

As far as I am concerned, this was the necessary outworking of Christian love in the fallen world as it is. The world is an abnormal world. Because of the Fall, it is not what God meant it to be. There are many things in this world which grieve us, but we must face them. We never have the luxury of acting in a merely utopian way. Utopian schemes in this fallen world have always brought tragedy. The Bible is never utopian.

Authentically biblical morality, and not a non-Christian and romantic counterfeit, demands that people have our prayers—but not *only* our prayers. It is biblical to say with General Bernard Rogers, supreme commander of allied forces in Europe, and a devout Baptist: "To have nuclear weapons in order to deter their use from the other side, to protect your people, that is moral, but I think it is immoral for a nation that is charged with that responsibility not to have the capability to deter that kind of war."[2]

We all grieve at any war, and especially at the prospect of nuclear war. But in a fallen world there are many things we grieve over but must nevertheless face. Since World War II, Europeans more than Americans have wanted the protection of nuclear weapons and have demanded this protection. Concerning the present deployment of United States Pershing II and cruise missiles in Western Europe, Helmut Schmidt said in the keynote speech at *Time*'s Atlantic Alliance Conference in May 1983: "We want the balance of military capabilities to be maintained. We saw that balance endangered by the enormous buildup of Soviet SS-20 missiles. I am responsible for the double-track decision as far as German participation goes, and I have not really changed my mind."[3]

The Europeans who are leaders in government have understood the reality of what Winston Churchill said immediately after World War II—that with their over-whelming forces the Soviets would easily dominate Western Europe if it were not for the deterrent of U.S. atomic weapons.

We have arrived at a crazy place, with a wild proliferation of nuclear weapons on both sides. Clearly there must be discussion here, and reduction of this capability if possible. But the fundamental factor has not changed: Europe, even more today than in Winston Churchill's day, would be under the threat of Soviet military and political domination if it were not for the existence of NATO's nuclear weaponry.

Incidentally, we may note that Europe's economic pros-perity—and some European nations now enjoy a higher standard of living than the United States—rests at least partly upon the fact that Europeans spend less for defense than they would have to spend if it were not for the U.S. nuclear presence. While the Soviets, with their lack of concern for the individual, have plowed huge proportions of their national income into building up their present gigantic military machine, Western Europe has been able to put less money into defense and more into economic build-up for the good of their people.

If the balance is now destroyed, there is no doubt in my mind that through either direct military action or political blackmail the greatly superior Soviet forces in Europe will soon overshadow Western Europe. It seems obtuse for anyone to fail to understand this, especially when all of the leaders of the European community, from conservatives to Socialists, see the only hope for continued safety and peace in Europe lying in Europe's maintaining the balance of both conventional and nuclear weapons. Speaking of the peace movement, even the ultraliberal Mr. Willy Brandt has said that he fears "the illusions which arise from being too far from reality. . . . Backing away from the NATO decision could give the Soviet Union an excuse for not negotiating seriously."[4]

Unilateral disarmament in this fallen world, especially in the face of aggressive Soviet materialism with its anti-God basis, would be altogether utopian and romantic. It would lead, as utopianism always does in this fallen world, to disaster. It may sound reasonable to talk of a freeze at the present level, or to say, "We won't ever use atomic weapons first." But if we think it through, either of these equals practical unilateral disarmament. To remove the nuclear deterrent in any effective sense would leave Europe at the mercy of the overwhelmingly superior Soviet forces in Europe. The Harvard University faculty group, in its 1983

book *Living With Nuclear Weapons,* is correct in saying that
"the danger of nuclear weapons lies in their use, rather than
their existence." It must not be forgotten, in this connection, that a freeze does not impose constraints on existing
weapons; no present guarantee of safety would be achieved
by such a measure.

Andrei Sakharov writing from his exile in Gorky speaks
against a freeze at the present level. He says in a letter
published in *Foreign Affairs* that:

> While the U.S.S.R. is the leader in this field [land-based
> missiles] there is very little chance of its easily relinquishing
> that lead. If it is necessary to spend a few billion dollars on
> MX missiles to alter this situation, then perhaps this is what
> the West must do.[5]

The world quite properly looks to the church in Germany
during the early days of Hitler's rise and curses it for not doing
something when something could have been done. Churchill remarked, in the House of Commons, after Chamberlain had signed the Munich Pact:

> [The people] should know that we have sustained a defeat
> without a war. . . . They should know that we have passed
> an awful milestone in our history . . . and that the terrible
> words have for the time being been pronounced against the
> Western democracies: "Thou art weighed in the balance
> and found wanting." And do not suppose this is the end;
> this is only the beginning of the reckoning. This is only the
> first sip, the first foretaste of a bitter cup which will be
> proffered to us year after year unless, by a supreme recovery
> of moral health and martial vigor, we arise again and take
> our stand for freedom as in olden times.

Who Is For Peace?

I do not always agree with the French political scientist and philosopher, Jacques Ellul; but he is certainly correct when he writes in his book, *False Presence of the Kingdom*:

> It was in 1930 that Christians should have alerted the world to decolonization, to Algeria and to Indochina. That is when the churches should have mobilized without letup. By 1956 those matters no longer held a shadow of interest. The socio-political process was already in operation, and it could not have made an iota of difference whether Christians got into the act or not. It would not have lessened a single atrocity nor resulted in a single act of justice. Likewise, it was in 1934 (the occupation of the Ruhr), or in 1935 (the war in Abyssinia), that Christians should have foretold the inevitable war against Nazism. That was when clarity of vision was essential. After 1937 it was too late. The fate of the world was already sealed for thirty years or more. But in those years the Christians, full of good intentions, were thinking only of peace and were loudly proclaiming pacifism! In matters of that kind, Christian good intentions are often disastrous.[6]

One can understand the romanticism of liberal theologians in these matters, since liberalism does not agree with the biblical stress on the fallen nature of this world. One can also understand the pacifism of the "peace churches": they have always taken Christ's command to individuals to turn the other cheek and misguidedly extended it to the state. They ignore the God-given responsibility of the state to protect its people and to stand for justice in a fallen world. Both of these points of view are understandable; but both are mistaken. If they carry the day and determine government policy, then the mistake will become a tragedy.

But when those who call themselves evangelical begin to

troop along in the popular, unthinking parade of our day, and begin to be romantic and utopian, it is time to speak openly in opposition. The May 30, 1983, issue of *Time* reports that the ambassador from the Vatican to Great Britain, Pro-Nuncio Bruno Heim, in a letter concerning Msgr. Bruce Kent, who leads the Campaign for Nuclear Disarmament in Britain, "suggested that the monsignor might be either an 'idiot' or a conscious agent of Soviet designs." The latter is probably not the case; however, one wonders if there is any explanation for the monsignor's attitude, or that of anyone who advocates what amounts to unilateral nuclear disarmament, other than some deficiency in his thinking.

If the peace marchers have been honestly confused as to the basic issues involved, their experience in Prague in June 1983 should enlighten them. While in Prague taking part in the Soviet-sponsored World Assembly for Peace and Life and Against Nuclear War, some members of the British Campaign for Nuclear Disarmament met with leaders of Charter 77, the Czech group which has tried to monitor the violations of the Helsinki Accords by the Soviet bloc. Quoting an editorial in the *Daily Telegraph* (London) of June 27, 1983: "British CND observers who saw the Czech security police descend on their meeting with representatives of the outlawed 'Charter 77' human rights group and rough up the Western media gained insight of a sort into the official mind of their hosts. Even Soviet propaganda has limits to its efficacy."

I am convinced that if Bible-believing people go along with the concept of "peace in our time" under the very plausible fear of nuclear war, which we all certainly share, then our children and grandchildren will quite properly curse us for not doing something at this moment to restrain Soviet expansion in Western Europe and other areas.

The threat of this expansion is not merely theoretical. We may consult the map if we are not clear as to what Soviet policy has gained for her during the last forty years. Naiveté, romanticism, and wishful thinking on our part can only mean more of the same; more of the world under this tyranny and also more of the world living in the horrible conditions which our brothers and sisters in Christ in the Soviet Union sustain. The denial of freedom there is not restricted to merely social or political freedoms: it means denial of the freedom to teach children about truth and about Christ. I do not want that for my children and my grandchildren. Nothing in the Bible tells me that I should want that for my children, whether they are my physical or my spiritual children.

In this connection we may cite some remarks from M. Quinlan, quoted in Jerram Barrs' book, *Peace and Justice in the Nuclear Age* (Crossway Books, Westchester, Ill.):

> The consequence of one-sided and unconditional nuclear renunciation is to leave us effectively defenceless against such a nuclear adversary. Renunciation then amounts to saying, in effect, that the right Christian response to the discovery of boundless military force is simply to leave the aggressive and the unscrupulous to wield it unopposed for any purposes they like, even if those turn out to be the purposes of Hitler or Stalin or Pol Pot.[7]

The issue at this moment, I believe, is nothing less than what we saw in the Churchill versus Chamberlain drama. We stand with one or the other.

The question comes down to this: which of us is really for peace, and which of us is for war? The realism of the Bible and the testimony of recent history leave us no doubt. Those whose position, either explicit or implicit, urges unilateral disarmament are with Chamberlain. They are for war, and at our moment of history that probably will include nuclear war. In contrast, I beseech you: Who among you is for peace?

1. John Train, "The Lonely Voice of Alexander Solzhenitsyn," *Wall Street Journal,* June 23, 1983.
2. Peter Nichols, "The General Is a Long Way from Apocalypse Now," *The Times* (London), Mar. 12, 1983, p. 86.
3. Helmut Schmidt, "A View Across the Atlantic," *Time,* May 9, 1983, p. 53.
4. *International Herald Tribune,* Apr. 20, 1982.
5. Andrei Sakharov, "The Danger of Thermonuclear War," *Foreign Affairs* 61, no. 5 (Summer 1983): 1013.
6. Jacques Ellul, *False Presence of the Kingdom* (New York: Seabury Press, 1972), pp. 187–88.
7. Jerram Barrs, *Peace and Justice in the Nuclear Age* (Greatham, New Hampshire: Garamond Press, 1983), p. 39.

The Peace Movement
&
the Soviet Union

by Vladimir Bukovsky

VLADIMIR BUKOVSKY *spent twelve years in Soviet prisons, work camps, and psychiatric hospitals before being released to the West in 1976 as a result of a public outcry. He recently graduated from Cambridge and now lives in California, where he is engaged in neuroscientific research at Stanford University. He is the author of an autobiographical book,* To Build a Castle: My Life as a Dissenter *(Viking, 1979) and, most recently, of* Cette lancinante douleur de la Liberté: Lettres d'un résistant russe aux Occidentaux *("This Stabbing Pain of Freedom: Letters of a Russian Resister to Westerners"), which was published in Paris in 1981.*

Peace will be preserved and strengthened if the people take the cause of peace into their own hands and defend it to the end.

JOSEPH STALIN, 1952

The "struggle for peace" has always been a cornerstone of Soviet foreign policy. Indeed, the Soviet Union itself rose out of the ashes of World War I under the banner of "Peace to the People! Power to the Soviets!" Probably from the very first, Bolshevik ideologists were aware of how powerful a weapon for them the universal craving for peace would be—how gullible and irrational people could be whenever they were offered the slightest temptation to believe that peace was at hand.

Only a year before the Bolsheviks raised their banner, the most terrible prospect for any Russian would have been to see an enemy burning down his villages and defiling his churches. Yet once blinded by the slogan, "A just peace without annexations or tribute," he was to rush from the front lines, along with hundreds of thousands of his fellow soldiers, sweeping away the last remnants of the Russian national state. He did not want to know that his desertion had done no more than simply prolong the war for another year, not only condemning thousands more to death on the Western front, but ending in that very German occupation of the Ukraine and Russia he had so much dreaded just a year ago. For the moment the only thing that mattered was peace—right now, and at any price.

Hardly anyone taking part in the stampede back home in

This article first appeared in *Commentary* magazine in May 1982. It is reprinted here with permission. All rights reserved.

1917 knew the first thing about the ideology of communism—except possibly for a couple of simple slogans and this one incendiary word: Peace. In a country of 170 million there were only 40,000 Communists. Anyone who had taken the trouble to read the Communists' "fine print" with just a little care could have discovered that what their soon-to-be masters meant by "peace" was not peace at all but rather the "transformation of imperialist war into civil war."

The Russian people were in any case so fed up with the war by then that they did not care. Anything seemed better, or at least not worse. After three years of civil war, however, in which some 20 million people were slaughtered or died of starvation, cold, and typhoid (i.e., *ten* times as many as were killed at the front during the whole of World War I), the war came to seem a trifle by comparison, a sort of frontier skirmish somewhere in the Byelorussian swamps.

And once again an irresistible craving for peace drove people to accept Soviet rule—as a lesser evil. Anything was now preferable to this monstrous slaughter, starvation, and typhoid. They would give anything for some kind of order.

The order imposed by the Communists was nothing more than a permanent state of civil war, both inside the country and around the world. Or as Lenin put it, as an ultimate objective peace simply means Communist world control. Thus, while Comrade Chicherin, at the Conference of Genoa in 1922, was appealing to the entire world for total and immediate disarmament, crowds of bewildered people in the Soviet Union were marching to the cheerful song:

> We'll fan the worldwide flame,
> Churches and prisons we'll raze to the ground.
> The Red Army is strongest of all
> From Moscow to the British islands.

Indeed, the churches were the first to be put to the torch. As for the prisons, the Communists were in no hurry to carry out their bold promise. Quite the contrary, the number of prisons grew with each year to accommodate tens of millions of "class enemies" or "enemies of the people." And speaking of worldwide flame, one need only compare the map of the world of, say, 1921 with that of 1981 to see that the song's promise was not entirely empty.

Once they recognized the power of "peace" as a weapon, the Communists have never let go of it. In this respect, it must be admitted, Soviet politics have invariably been most "peaceful." We must at the same time bear in mind that according to Communist dogma, wars are the "inevitable consequence of the clash of imperialist interests under capitalism," and therefore they will continue to be inevitable as long as capitalism exists. The only way to save humanity from the evil of wars, then, is to "liberate" it from the "chains of capitalism." Accordingly, there is a very precise distinction to be made between "just wars" and "unjust wars." "Just wars" are those fought "in the interests of the proletariat." It is perfectly simple and perfectly clear: just wars are absolutely justifiable because they lead to the creation of a world in which there will be no wars, forevermore. Proletarians are all brothers, are they not? So, once the world is rid of capitalists, imperialists, and various other class enemies, why should those who are left fight one another?

By this same impeccable logic, the interests of the proletariat are best known to the advance-guard of the proletariat, that is, the Communist party, and should be defined by Lenin, Stalin, Khrushchev, and Brezhnev, since they are in turn the advance-guard of the Communist party.

As soon as we have pinned down this formula and deciphered its terminology, the course of history becomes absolutely clear. For instance, Soviet occupation of the Baltic states and Bessarabia, or the war with Finland in 1939–40, were of course perfectly just, as was the partition of Poland, achieved in cooperation with Nazi Germany in 1939. On the other hand, the Nazi attack on the Soviet Union in 1941 was blatantly unjust. By the same token, any attack by the Arabs on Israel is just, at least insofar as it is successful. If Israeli resistance to attack is successful, however, then all peace-loving peoples must protest.

It goes without saying that world public opinion must accept the distinction I have outlined above and direct every effort in the struggle for peace toward establishing it. Fortunately, there are a great many "progressive" people in the world, people for whom any direction taken by Moscow is progressive because by definition it is taken in the service of socialism. Thus, before the Molotov-Ribbentrop Pact of 1939 was signed, the energies of all progressive people were mobilized against fascism, whether in Spain, Italy, or Germany. As soon as the pact was signed, the notion of what was progressive and what was not changed drastically. [1]

On February 2, 1940, for example, the German Communist leader, Walter Ulbricht, later to become head of the East German state, published an article in *Die Welt* in which he said: "Those who intrigue against the friendship of the German and Soviet peoples are enemies of the German people and are branded as accomplices of British imperialism."

The British *Daily Worker* adopted a similar line and greeted the new alliance as a victory for peace, as did the American *Daily Worker.* On September 19, 1939, when the war was raging in Poland, it published a declaration of the National Committee of the American Communist party proclaiming the war declared by France and Britain on Nazi Germany to be an imperialist (that is, "unjust") one, which should be opposed by the workers. This appeal was immediately supported by fellow-travelers like Theodore Dreiser, and Communist trade unions set out to sabotage production in munitions factories, lest any aid reach Britain or France. Right up to the eve of the Nazi invasion of Russia, Communist propaganda did everything possible to dissuade the United States from helping the European democracies in their war against Nazi Germany. These pages in the history of the glorious "struggle for peace" by the progressive social forces are not much spoken of any more, particularly where the young might hear.

But nowhere was this "struggle for peace" as influential as in France, where the Communist party and its fellow-travelers were openly defeatist before, and remained so during—and some time after—the Nazi invasion of France. The French Communist party, which was quite considerable in strength, worked so energetically to undermine the French war effort as to suggest a fifth column. Within a month of France's declaration of war the party's leader, Maurice Thorez, fled to Moscow to direct the resistance to French preparations against Germany. In November 1940 Thorez and his associate Jacques Duclos exulted openly over the fall of France, Thorez declaring that "the struggle of the French people has the same aim as the struggle of German imperialism."

The Franco-German alliance alluded to by Thorez expressed itself in concrete terms. German propaganda leaflets dropped over the Maginot line pointed out that "Germany, after her victory over Poland and since her pact with Russia, disposes of inexhaustible resources in men and material," while all the Communist deputies petitioned

President Herriot to make peace in response to Hitler's appeal. After Communist publications had been suspended by decree in France, the party continued to publish its propaganda on German presses. Its leaflets urged troops, dockers, and others engaged in essential war work to resist and to sabotage the country's effort. In March 1940, a party leaflet claimed that the Allied failure to launch an offensive was due to the effectiveness of the party's defeatist propaganda. And there can be no doubt that this effective spreading of defeatism, coupled with a serious campaign of sabotage in munitions factories, played a major role in the catastrophic French defeat of June 1940.

At the very time that General de Gaulle, in London, was issuing his appeal for resistance, the French Communist paper *l'Humanité* said: "General de Gaulle and other agents of British capital would like to compel Frenchmen to fight for the City. . . ."

Later Khrushchev was to recall that "Stalin once told me that Hitler had sent a request for a favor through secret channels. Hitler wanted Stalin, as the man with the most authority and prestige in the Communist world, to persuade the French Communists not to lead the resistance against the German occupation of France." Evidently Hitler's request was not denied.

Even in Yugoslavia, where the Communist movement had directed all its efforts to vilifying the British and French, Tito's first appeal for a struggle against the German invaders did not come until June 22, 1941. It was not the German conquest of Yugoslavia that aroused his ire, but the German invasion of the Soviet Union. Even in far-off Buenos Aires, a British diplomat had noticed that Nazi diplomats were "collaborating with local Communists in a very dangerous attempt to win over the masses with the cry of 'away with British capitalism and commercial exploitation.'"

As soon as Nazi Germany turned against its great Eastern ally, the "struggle for peace" was instantly terminated. Indeed, the sudden outburst of patriotism among the "progressive social forces" was remarkable. No strikes, no condemnation of Western imperialism—as if the latter had never existed. For the remainder of World War II the Allies were to enjoy a happy time of industrial peace and a relaxation of the class struggle. The war, of course, was now a "just" one.

Oddly, the passion for peace was resurrected shortly after the war was over, while the Soviet Union was swallowing a dozen countries in Central Europe and threatening to engulf the rest of the continent. At that time, some "imperialist warmongers" were sounding the alarm over Soviet conduct and even suggesting the creation of a "very aggressive" NATO alliance. The "reactionary forces" in the world were starting a "cold war." Beyond this, the Soviet Union was troublesomely lagging behind the United States in the development of nuclear weapons. For some curious reason, however, the "imperialist military-industrial complex"—all those Dr. Strangeloves—failed to drop the atom bomb on Moscow while they still enjoyed a monopoly on it. This should undoubtedly be ascribed to the success of a great movement of peace-lovers. How could it be explained otherwise, short of the reactionary suggestion that NATO generals were not in the least aggressive?

In any case, members of the older generation can still remember the marches, the rallies, and the petitions of the 1950s (particularly the famous Stockholm Appeal and the meetings of the indefatigable World Peace Council). It is hardly a secret now that the whole campaign was organized, conducted, and financed from Moscow, through the so-called Peace Fund and the Soviet-dominated World Peace

Council—where a safe majority was secured by such figures as Ilya Ehrenburg, A.N. Tikhonov, etc. This was the period when Comrade Stalin presented his memorable recipe for peace that is the epigraph to this article. Stalin's formulation was enthusiastically taken up by millions, some of them Communists, some loyal fellow-travelers, a number of them muddleheaded intellectuals, or hypocrites seeking popularity, or clerics hungry for publicity—not to mention professional campaigners, incorrigible fools, youths eager to rebel against anything, and outright Soviet agents. Surprisingly, this odd mixture constitutes a fairly sizable population in any Western society, and in no time at all the new peace campaign had reached grandiose proportions. It became fashionable to join it and rather risky to decline.

The purpose of all this peace pandemonium was well calculated in the Kremlin. First, the threat of nuclear war (of which the Soviets periodically created a reminder by fomenting an international crisis) combined with the scope of the peace movement should both frighten the bourgeoisie and make it more tractable. Second, the recent Soviet subjugation of Central European countries should be accepted with more serenity by Western public opinion and quickly forgotten. Third, the movement should help to stir up anti-American sentiment among the Europeans, along with a mistrust of their own governments, thus moving the political spectrum to the Left. Fourth, it should make military expenditures and the placement of strategic nuclear weapons so unpopular, so politically embarrassing, that in the end the process of strengthening Western defenses would be considerably slowed, giving the Soviets crucial time to catch up. Fifth, since the odd mixture of fools and knaves described above is usually drawn from the most socially active element in the population, its activism should be given the right direction.

The results were to exceed all expectations. Soviet money had clearly been well spent. The perception of the Soviet Union as an ally of the West (rather than of Nazi Germany) was still fresh in peoples' minds, which undoubtedly contributed to the success of the "struggle for peace."

Subsequently, the death of Stalin, the shock created by the official disclosure of his crimes, the Khrushchev "thaw" in international relations, and, above all, the fact that the Soviets had caught up with the West in nuclear weapons, were to make the peace movement temporarily redundant; it ceased to exist just as suddenly as it had once appeared. Meanwhile, the inefficiency of the Soviet economy once again brought it to the point of collapse. The Soviet Union badly needed Western goods, technology, and credits. Without these, there would have to be very substantial economic reform, dangerous to continued party control over the entire economic life of the Soviet Union. At the same time, it was from the strategic point of view important for the Soviets to legitimize their territorial holdings in Eastern Europe and to secure for themselves the freedom to move further. Something new was called for. Out of the depths of the Kremlin, the doctrine of détente was born.

Though the peace movement was put in cold storage, the issue of peace was nevertheless central to this new Kremlin policy as well. The West had grown so exhausted by the constant tension of the previous decades that the temptation to relax, when offered by the Kremlin, was simply irresistible. And after a decade of a ruthless "struggle for peace," no Western government could get away with rejecting a proposal to limit the arms race—however well some of them understood that it would be senseless to try to reach an agreement with the Soviets while the essentially aggressive nature of Communist power remained in force

Probably some such recognition explains why the Western governments insisted on linking participation in the Helsinki agreements to the observance of human-rights agreements inside the Communist bloc. Their idea was to force the internal relaxation of the Soviet regime and so make it more open and less aggressive. In exchange the West provided almost everything Brezhnev demanded in his "Peace Program" of the 24th Party Congress in 1971. "The inviolability of the postwar frontiers in Europe"—that is, the legitimation of the Soviet territorial annexations between 1939 and 1948—as well as a substantial increase in economic, scientific, and cultural cooperation were solemnly granted by the Western countries in Helsinki in 1975. Earlier a separate treaty had perpetuated the artificial division of Germany without even a reference to the Berlin Wall.

The Western democracies had displayed such readiness to accommodate their Soviet partners that their behavior was perceived as weakness. Probably the most disgusting features of détente could be seen in Germany where the "free flow of people and ideas" had very quickly degenerated into trading people like cattle, the right to visit one's relatives in the East becoming a kind of reward conditional on the "good behavior" of the West German government. By playing on this sensitive issue the Soviets were able to blackmail the whole country and to "modify" the policies of its government. Unfortunately, Germany is a key factor in East-West relations because in order to avoid a major split in the Western alliance the other members have to adjust their positions in accordance with Germany's. So it was that Soviet influence came to be exerted through the back door, and the West was politically paralyzed.

In addition, far from making the Soviets more dependent—as the proponents of détente had assured us—increased trade, and particularly huge Western credits, have made the West more and more dependent on the Soviet Union. The dimensions of this disaster became clear only recently, when the discussion of economic sanctions against the Polish military rulers and their Soviet masters revealed the inability of the Western countries to reduce once-established economic relations with the Eastern bloc without harming themselves even more. In fact, by now the Soviets are in a position to threaten the *West* with economic sanctions. Undoubtedly, they will take advantage of it very soon.

In the meantime, far from relaxing internally, the Soviet regime had stepped up its repressive policies, totally ignoring the weak Western protests against Soviet violations of the human-rights agreements. The weakness of these protests had in turn served only as further incitement for the Soviets to proceed in their course of repression without restraint. Clearly, the ideological war waged by the Soviets through all those earlier years had only increased in intensity during the era of détente. Nor did they try to camouflage this warfare. On the contrary, Leonid Brezhnev stated openly in his speech to the 25th Party Congress, on February 24, 1977: ". . . it is clear as can be that détente and peaceful coexistence relate to interstate relations. Détente in no way rescinds, or can rescind, the laws of the class struggle."

Furthermore, as it transpired, instead of reducing their military expenditures and arms build-up, as the Western nations had during those years, the Soviet Union, taking advantage of Western relaxation, had significantly increased its arsenal. So much so that if in the 1960s it could be said that a certain parity between East and West had been achieved, by now the Soviets have reached a point of clear advantage over the West. We also now know that the benefits to the Soviet Union of trade with the West were invariably put to military use. For example, the Kama River truck factory built by Americans in the 1970s has recently begun manufacturing the military trucks that were observed in action during the Soviet invasion of Afghanistan.

By the end of the 1970s the West was becoming increasingly aware of these dangerous developments. The usefulness of détente, long challenged by some, was now being questioned by many. And then came the final blow—on Christmas 1979. Just at the moment when most people in the West were preoccupied with such things as Christmas cards and presents, something like 100,000 Soviet soldiers moved in to occupy neighboring Afghanistan, an officially "nonaligned" country with a population of about 17 million. The world was shocked and the USSR was immediately placed in isolation. Even the Communist parties of many countries condemned the Soviet action as a piece of blatant aggression. The invasion of Afghanistan, followed by the arbitrary banishment to internal exile of Nobel laureate Andrei Sakharov, followed still later by the threatening of Poland (leading, finally, to the imposition of martial law), virtually terminated the era of détente.

This termination has cost the Soviets dearly. In fact, they have lost almost everything they had gradually managed to gain while the West was enjoying its bout of unilateral relaxation. Ratification of the SALT II agreement was suspended indefinitely. The Americans were awakened from their prolonged lethargy to discover with horror how weak, ineffective, and unproductive their country had become. In this new psychological atmosphere, the victory of Ronald Reagan was inevitable, promising an end to American defense cutbacks, the deployment of a new, previously shelved, generation of weapons like the B-1 bomber, the cruise missile, the MX, and the neutron bomb. It seemed equally inevitable that the military budgets of all the other Western countries would be increased, while the trade, technology, and credit arrangements with the Soviets would be reduced, or at least be made more difficult to obtain.

Thus, if this trend were to continue, the Soviets would lose their position of military superiority—especially in view of the fact that their economy is so much less efficient than that of "rotten capitalism." Add to this the new wave of international hostility noticeable especially in the Muslim world (the United Nations General Assembly voted against the Soviets on Afghanistan, for the first time since the Korean war), a continuing crisis in Poland, a hopeless war in Afghanistan, and a growing unrest among the population at home caused by food shortages, and the picture grew so gloomy as to be just short of disaster. Clearly the Soviet rulers had to undertake something dramatic to avoid a total catastrophe.

I myself, to tell the truth, was not very much surprised when suddenly, within a year, a mighty peace movement came into being in Western Europe. Especially since, by some strange coincidence, this movement showed itself first of all precisely in those European countries where the old missiles were to be replaced by newer Pershings and cruise missiles. I make no claim to special prescience; it is just that after thirty-four years of life in my beloved Communist motherland, I have some sense of its government's bag of tricks, pranks, and stunts. In fact, it was not a very difficult thing to predict, for the Soviet state is not a particularly intelligent creature. If you think of it rather as a huge, brainless, antediluvian reptile with a more or less fixed set of

47

reflexes, you cannot go far wrong. "Well, here we are, back to the 1950s again," I thought to myself.

What was much more amusing to observe was the ease with which presumably mature and responsible people had by the thousands fallen into the Soviet booby trap. It is as if history were repeating itself before our eyes, offering us a chance to see how the Russian state collapsed in 1917, or how France collapsed within one month in 1940. It is also quite amusing, if one has a taste for such amusement, to be reminded of how people are practically incapable of deriving any useful knowledge from even the recent lessons of history. Once again, the universal craving for peace right now, this very moment, and at any price, has rendered people utterly illogical and irrational, and left them simply unable to think calmly. Their current arguments, if one may call them that, are so childish, senseless, selfish, that an involuntary smile comes immediately to one's lips. Even at best what one hears is a parroting of the kind of old moldy Soviet slogans and clichés that even schoolchildren in the Soviet Union would laugh at.

To begin with, why is it that everyone nas suddenly begun to be so apprehensive about nuclear war again? What has happened to make it more real than it was, say, two or three years ago? The entire history of East-West relations shows that the only way to force the Soviets to respect agreements is to deal from a position of strength. So are we to understand that because the Soviets might cease to be militarily superior to us, nuclear war is once again a reality? Should we, then, take this proposition to its logical conclusion and say that the only guarantee of peace is Soviet military superiority?

Meanwhile, countless TV programs have suddenly sprung up that unfold before us images of the great treasures of our civilization—paintings, sculptures, pyramids, antiquities, etc.—and at the end of each the narrator reminds us, his voice trembling with noble passion, how terrible it would be if all these treasures were to be destroyed along with the great civilization that produced them. And on other channels, we are treated to documentary after documentary about nuclear explosions and the consequences of radiation. After such relentless programming, naturally public-opinion polls show a sudden increase in the number of those who believe that nuclear war is imminent.

Then there is the catchy new idea that "Our deterrent does not deter anymore." Why? Has a nuclear war begun already? Have the Soviets attacked any NATO country? Or is it simply because those who like to say the deterrent no longer deters have seen their full quota of televised nuclear explosions?

It is so easy to start a panic. The question is: who is served by this panic? The Soviet-controlled World Peace Council declared in 1980 (and the whole European peace movement repeats it as if under a hypnotic spell): "The people of the world are alarmed. Never before has there been so great a danger of a world nuclear holocaust. The nuclear arms build-up, the accumulation of deadly arsenals, has reached a critical point. Further escalation in the arms build-up could create a most dangerous situation, facing humanity with the threat of annihilation."

Never before. But was not the world in as much danger a year earlier? The leaders of the European peace movement themselves claim that the nuclear potential accumulated on both sides is sufficient for them to destroy one another ten times. Is there any technical reason why "twenty times" is more dangerous than, say, "five times"? Or is it that, like a nuclear charge itself, the accumulation must reach a "critical mass" in order to explode?

Somehow, in the midst of all this nuclear hysteria it seems

to be totally forgotten that bombs themselves are quite harmless, unless somebody wishes to drop them. So why are we suddenly alarmed by the stockpile of hardware and not by the Soviet military move toward the Persian Gulf?

Again, quite suddenly, voices begin to cry out in a huge chorus, "Nuclear weapons are immoral!" Wait a minute. Did these weapons just become immoral? Are conventional weapons moral? Why should this idea come all at once into the minds of so many people? Take as another example the question of the new missiles to be deployed in Europe. Why is it more dangerous to replace the old missiles with the new ones than to leave the old ones where they are? Are not the old ones equipped with nuclear warheads as well? To be sure, the new missiles are more accurate. So what? We can thank God that they are on our side. They may make life more difficult for the Kremlin adventurers, but why should millions of people in the West perceive that as a tragedy and danger?

Deep in their hearts most of these terrified people have a very simple answer to all these "whys." They know that the only real source of danger is the Soviet Union and that anything which might make the Soviets angry is dangerous for that very reason. But fear is a paralyzing and deranging force, so deranging as to lead some people to advocate the abolition of the police because the criminals are becoming too aggressive.

Indeed, the most amazing aspect of the present antiwar hysteria—aside from the fact that it has arisen at a time so remarkably favorable for Moscow—is the direction of the campaign. Millions of people in Great Britain, Germany, Holland, Belgium, France, and Italy, supposedly of sound mind and with no evidence of the influence of LSD, march about claiming that the threat of war comes from . . . their own governments and the government of the United States!

A psychoanalyst might characterize this behavior as the Freudian replacement of a real object of fear with an imaginary one. Except that even a psychoanalyst might conclude that pro-Soviet propaganda had something to do with the delusion in this particular case.

The facts are too obvious to discuss here. One may like or dislike President Reagan or Chancellor Schmidt, but unlike Comrade Brezhnev, they were elected by the majority of their respective populations and are fully accountable in their actions to the parliaments and to the people. They simply cannot declare a war on their own. Besides, it is quite enough to look around to see the real source of aggression. Was it American or Soviet troops who occupied half of Germany and built a wall in Berlin? Is it not the Soviets who still occupy Hungary, Czechoslovakia, the Baltic states, not to mention Afghanistan, very much against the wishes of the people in these countries? Was it East or West German troops who took part in the occupation of Czechoslovakia and who are prepared to invade Poland?

Everything in the West is done quite openly—one might say, far too openly. But what do we know about the decisions made by fourteen old fools in the Politburo whom nobody ever elected to make these decisions and whom nobody can call to account? No press is allowed to criticize them, no demonstrations to protest against their dictate. Anyone refusing to obey their secret orders would instantly disappear forever. There is in fact very little difference between the Soviet system and that of Nazi Germany. Is there anyone who supposes that he should have trusted Hitler more than the democracies?

After the experience of speaking several times with members of the current European peace movement, however, I know only too well how futile is the recourse to rational argument. They announce unabashedly that there is no Soviet military superiority. It is all, they say, CIA propaganda; the only reliable source of information as far as they are concerned seems to be the KGB. They refer one to the findings of a certain Stockholm International Peace Research Institute, leaving one to guess at the kind of methods employed by this institute for assessing the Soviet arsenal. Since the Institute has no satellites at its disposal, its "researchers" are undoubtedly left in a painful dilemma: whether to obtain their information from the blue sky, or from the Sputniks. Nobody in the European peace movement, it seems, has ever wondered about the reliability of this obscure establishment.

But this is just a trifle. More seriously, our peace-lovers—repeating word for word an old *Pravda* cliché—maintain that the "crazy American generals" are so trigger-happy as to push the button just for the fun of it. I have never been able to understand why generals must invariably be crazy—American generals, of course, not the Soviet kind, who seem to have some innate immunity from craziness—and if they are crazy, why they did not push the damn button long ago. In any case, it is hard to imagine that the generals, who at least have some technical education, are less equipped to understand nuclear problems than the primary-school teachers who are so heavily represented in the peace movement.

Some of the "peacemakers" sincerely believe that as soon as the West disarms itself, the Soviets will follow suit, and with an almost literally incredible naiveté they urge us to "try" this suicidal experiment. Others, far more sophisticated, know perfectly well that their Soviet comrades need to gain time so as to enjoy a more advantageous posture in future negotiations with the Americans. What they urge is that the West start negotiations first and improve the Western position later. Still others are more candidly selfish and object only to the deployment of nuclear weapons near their own village, so to speak—as if being protected is more dangerous than not being protected. Or better still, as if any single village, city, or country could maintain neutrality during a nuclear war. "Let the Americans fight the Russians," they say, implying that the entire problem of the modern world grows out of some stupid far-off quarrel between "Americans and Russians," who are apparently in some kind of conspiracy to destroy the poor Europeans. Surely if Comrade Brezhnev promised to respect the "nuclear-free zones" in case of war, people could heave a sigh of relief and go to sleep untroubled. If Brezhnev says so, there will be no nuclear-armed submarines off your shores. After all, has Comrade Brezhnev ever broken his word? Of course not. He is an honest man. He is so honest he can even guarantee you in what direction the contaminated clouds will move and locate for you the radioactive fallout. "Why should the Russians attack us, if we are disarmed?" Why indeed? Ask the Afghan peasants, they would probably know the answer.

There is no sense in rehearsing all the various "peace arguments," so contradictory and even incompatible that one wonders how those who make them manage to get along together in the same movement. Only one thing these various strands have in common: panic, and a readiness to capitulate to the Soviet threat even before such capitulation is demanded. Better red than dead. That is why current Soviet propaganda has so quickly become so remarkably successful.

Indeed, it is difficult to imagine a more openly pro-Soviet line than that of the European peace movement.[2] It is even more pro-Soviet than that of the local Communist parties, who after all at least have to camouflage themselves with a cover of independence from Moscow. Nothing is more obvious, for example, than that the present increase in international tension was brought about by the Soviet invasion of Afghanistan. There is hardly a country, a political party (including some Communist parties), or an international organization that did not condemn the Soviet aggression unequivocally. The only public movement in Western Europe that never condemned the invasion, paradoxically, is the one that calls itself the "peace movement." No such condemnation has ever been pronounced at a peace-movement rally in Western Europe, or passed as a resolution, or published in one of the movement's major publications, or circulated as a mass petition. Perhaps you will imagine that the peace groups condemned the invasion in their hearts? On the contrary, the evidence is far more convincing that they simply justify this international crime.

Not long ago I myself was publicly charged by the leaders of the British Campaign for Nuclear Disarmament (CND) with having distorted their position on Afghanistan. Therefore I find it particularly useful to quote from an official CND booklet, *Why We Need Action, Not Words,* by Betty England: "The intervention in Afghanistan may well have been caused partly by the Soviet Union's fear of its growing encirclement. The fear cannot be called unreasonable after Sir Neil Cameron's statement in Peking . . ." (p. 12). In other words, the poor Russians whom Sir Neil, Marshal of the Royal Air Force, so frightened with a speech critical of them, must have good reason for what they do. By this logic, we ought to be imposing strict censorship on anti-Soviet speeches lest we be faced with Soviet occupation of the entire world. But the implications are even more important. The idea buried in Miss England's passage is that the only way to keep the peace is gradually to accept the Soviet system and Soviet demands.

Even more outspoken than the CND is the World Peace Council. Its booklet, *Program of Action 1981*, contains a direct instruction to support the present puppet government of Afghanistan (p. 25). This program was *unanimously* adopted in 1980 by a gathering in Sofia, Bulgaria, of representatives of most of the peace groups (about this gathering, more later). After this it comes as no surprise that at the recent International Peace Conference in Denmark it was decided to convene the next meeting in Kabul, the capital of Afghanistan, within six months.

It is obvious that a Soviet invasion of Poland would bring us closer to world war or, to be more precise, would make any real relaxation of international tension quite impossible for ten or fifteen years. And once again, the only public movement that has never condemned the continuous Soviet threat to Poland (and is still uncertain about its reaction to the Soviet-dictated imposition of martial law) is the peace movement. The leaders of the biggest British peace group, CND, went even further, publicly praising themselves for not "overreacting" to the events in Poland (B. Kent, letter to the London *Times*, December 9, 1981) only a few days before the imposition of martial law, and displaying their "impartiality" by equating the Polish crisis with that in East Timor. Perhaps the leaders of the movement seeking to promote peace in Europe should be reminded that in 1975 the thirty-five countries of Europe, together with Canada and the U.S., solemnly recognized an inseparable link between security in Europe and respect for human rights in the participating countries. Should we assume that the CND leadership refuses to accept the Helsinki agreement, or are we to conclude that it is indifferent to the question of European security?

At least about Poland not all in the movement can be accused of indifference. I have, for instance, never heard of a case in which a representative of the Chilean or Argentinean government was invited to expound his government's views before any international peace conference. But for some strange reason, an exception was recently made for a representative of the Polish junta, who was invited by the World Peace Council to address the International Peace Conference in Denmark. His vicious lies about Solidarity and personal slanders against Lech Walesa (see the *Guardian*, January 11, 1982) were greeted with hearty applause by the peace-lovers (BBC report).

It is simple common sense to try to restrain both sides of any would-be conflict if one wishes to preserve peace. But the European peace movement is so remarkably unilateral that it seems barely conscious of "the other side." It cries shame on the Americans for as yet nonexistent weapons like the neutron bomb, or the not-yet-deployed cruise and Pershing missiles, but speaks only in whispers, if that, of the hundreds of Soviet SS-20s already aimed at Europe.

Since, again, I have provoked an angry reaction from the CND leaders for pointing out this particular instance of extreme unilateralism (London *Times*, December 9, 1981), I looked through the major CND publications once more. The booklet by Betty England quoted above does not contain a single mention of the SS-20s, though it is virtually saturated with the names of American missiles. Nor does a widely distributed report on the CND annual conference of 1981 (the latest to my knowledge), nor the official CND leaflet, *Nuclear War and You,* dropped into my mailbox by some caring hand. Only recently I have learned that a decision to mention the SS-20 was finally taken by CND after many heated debates and very much against the wishes of the CND leadership, many of whom are also members of the British Communist party.

Oddly enough, there are many in the European peace movement who have worked (some still do) with Amnesty International in support of prisoners of conscience in the Communist countries. Unfortunately, this by itself does not seem to prevent one from making dangerous political mistakes, nor, to judge from the results, does it guarantee any moderating influence on the movement's leadership. Be that as it may, the fact is that the European peace movement (including its large constituent organizations) has never said a word in support of the thousands of people in the USSR who are imprisoned for opposing aggressive Soviet policies, for refusing to serve in the army on errands of aggression, or refusing to shoot civilians in Afghanistan. During all the time that thousands of "peace-lovers" were noisily expressing their one-sided feelings on the streets of London, Bonn, Amsterdam, and Brussels, not one word was said about Sakharov, still in exile and on a hunger strike—Sakharov, who has done more than anyone in the world to halt nuclear testing. These peaceful souls would happily throw stones at General Haig, but they would welcome Marshal Brezhnev with servile smiles.

This is not to deny that there are plenty of well-intentioned, and genuinely concerned and frightened people in the movement's ranks. I am certain that the overwhelming majority of them are. Just as it did in the 1950s, the movement today probably consists of the same odd mixture of Communists, fellow-travelers, muddleheaded intellectuals, hypocrites seeking popularity, professional political speculators, frightened bourgeois, and youths eager to rebel just for the sake of rebelling. There are also the inevitable Catholic priests with a "mission" and other religious people who believe that God has chosen them to make peace on earth right now. But there is also not the slightest doubt that this motley crowd is manipulated by a handful of scoundrels instructed directly from Moscow.

In fact, just as this essay was going to press, John Vinocur reported in the New York *Times* (April 6, 1982) "the first public substantiation from inside the antinuclear movement . . . that the West German Communist party, at the direction of the Soviet Union, has attempted to coopt public sentiment against nuclear weapons." The environmentalist party known as the Greens "charged that the West German Communist party, which is aligned with Moscow, dominated and manipulated a meeting [in Bonn] Sunday [April 4] in which representatives of 37 groups, describing themselves as elements of the antimissile movement, planned a major demonstration against President Reagan when he visits Bonn . . . June 10." The Greens, who participated in the meeting, acknowledge that they themselves have cooperated with the Communists "on certain local issues," but what happened in Bonn was "scandalous" even to them. "The Communists dominated the meeting completely. It took place under seemingly democratic rules, but that was a joke. We could barely get a word in." The meeting—at which were represented such groups as the German Student Federation, the Evangelical Student Committee, the Federation of German Youth Groups, and the German Peace Society— rejected resolutions condemning Soviet interference in Poland and Soviet intervention in Afghanistan, and the delegates refused to express support for Solidarity. "They adopted, however, by a large majority, a motion condemning

United States actions in Central America, the Middle East, southern Africa, and other regions."

Earlier, as I was in the process of writing this essay, news came that one of the Danish leaders of the movement, Arne Petersen, was arrested along with his wife for channeling Soviet money into the funds of the peace movement. His master, the Second Secretary of the Soviet embassy in Copenhagen, was expelled from the country. Now and then we hear about subsidized trips taken by peace activists to the best Soviet resorts where they are wined and dined royally— and, of course, shown kindergartens, schools, and hospitals (no munitions factories).

The majority of the European peace movement are undoubtedly not aware of these facts. Probably they will ignore the charges of the Greens, just as they missed the reports of Mr. Petersen's activities, which involved placing paid advertisements (out of Soviet donations) for the Danish peace movement in the Danish papers, ads signed by a number of prominent Danish intellectuals (who for sure knew nothing about it). And even our angry CND leaders "know nothing of the subsidized trips to Soviet resorts" (London *Times*, December 9, 1981). Well, sometimes it is very comfortable—even for professional intellectuals—not to know things. . . .

For those, however, who do wish to know, let us track down the origin of the current revival of the "struggle for peace." Anyone who has read thus far will not be surprised to hear that the earliest traces of this revival are to be found in Soviet publications, quite clear for those who know how to read them:

The first bright colors of autumn have already touched the emerald green parks of Sofia. The golden leaves of maples and aspens are trembling on the breeze. And everywhere the tender-blue streamers bearing the insignia of the World Peace Council. Sofia is expecting an important event: the World Parliament of the Peoples for Peace will be working here from 23 to 27 of September. It is the biggest and the most representative meeting of the world's peace forces convened in the last years by the World Peace Council (*Izvestia*, September 23, 1980).

The same day *Pravda* referred to "the biggest gathering in history of the fighters for peace." Indeed, the most peaceful and independent country of the world, Bulgaria, played host during those September days to 2,260 peace-lovers from 137 countries, claiming to represent 330 political parties, 100 international and over 3,000 national nongovernmental organizations. To be sure, this was no ordinary meeting of the international Communist movement. The political spectrum of those represented was exceptionally wide: 200 members of different national parliaments, 200 trade-union leaders, 129 leading Social Democrats (33 of them members of their respective national executive bodies), 150 writers and poets, 33 representatives of different liberation movements (including the Association in Defense of Civil Rights from Northern Ireland), women's organizations (like the National Assembly of British Women), youth organizations, the World Council of Churches and other religious organizations, 18 representatives of different UN specialized committees and commissions, representatives of the Organization of African Unity and of OPEC, ex-military people, some of them generals, and representatives of 83 Communist parties (*Pravda*, September 23, 24, 25, 26, 27, 28, 29, November 5, 1980; *Izvestia*, September 23, 24, 27, 28, 1980).

It had all started about a year earlier, as we are informed by a talkative Bulgarian, the chairman of the Organizational Bureau, responsible for the "practical preparation" for this show (*Pravda*, September 23, 1980). They had expected, you see, only 1,500 delegates, but 2,200 came. No wonder the chairman wished to talk about his success.

Yet a year earlier—in 1979—none of the conditions now cited to explain the current miraculous resurrection of the peace movement existed. There was no so-called "new strategy of the Pentagon," the famous presidential directive 59; there was no new escalation of the arms race; there was no neutron bomb. The Vienna summit meeting had just been successfully concluded with the signing of SALT II. September 1979 was a time of universal happiness, the sky was cloudless. Only one significant thing happened in September 1979: a sudden wave of mass arrests in the Soviet Union and, as we have learned now, a decision to reactivate the peace movement. Who could have predicted in September 1979 that within a year the Cold War would be back—who else but those involved in "practical preparations" for the invasion of Afghanistan? Given the nature of the Soviet planned economy, with its fabulously inflexible, slow, and inefficient workings, the Soviets must prepare everything well in advance. Why should they have allocated such a large sum of money to hold a Bulgarian peace show in the middle of happy times, if not in anticipation of grave political trouble ahead?

Furthermore, we learn from Comrade Zhivkov, the Bulgarian Communist leader who opened the meeting with a long speech, about an appropriate decision taken by the Political Consultative Committee of the Warsaw Bloc countries in May 1980 (*Pravda*, September 24, 1980), as well as an appropriate resolution of the Plenary Session of the Central Committee in June 1980 (*Pravda*, September 29,

1980). Comrade Zhivkov was simply revealing the way decisions and resolutions first travel through the Communist bureaucratic machinery on their way to rubberstamping by a "representative" body—in this case, the Sofia "Parliament" in September.

Indeed, the whole show was depressingly familiar to anyone acquainted with the methods the Kremlin producers applied to the same scenario in the time of Stalin. Even the dramatis personae were the same. There was the same World Peace Council with its immortal President Ramesh Chandra; there was the same chief conductor, Boris Ponomarev, former official of the Comintern (now responsible in the Politburo for contacts with fraternal Communist parties as well as for intelligence). Even the slogan adopted for the occasion, "The people have the power to preserve peace—their basic right," was remarkably similar to the unforgettable words of Comrade Stalin in 1952.

Only this time the personal message that Comrade Ponomarev brought to those convened was from Comrade Brezhnev, not Comrade Stalin. The latter, of course, would never have tolerated even the mention of the term *rights*—basic or any other—in his slogans. Well, the times have changed after all. Still, those damned "human rights" had gotten out of hand. Hence, better to find something like "basic rights."

The first to speak, as I said, was Comrade Zhivkov, and he spilled the beans about the Soviets' real concern (*Pravda*, September 24, 1980). The aggressive circles in America, he said, refuse to accept the present balance of forces in the world. They don't wish to submit to their historically predestined defeat. They have become so arrogant as to reject all of the recent Soviet peace proposals. They have decided to replace détente with a policy based on a "position of strength." They don't observe agreements on cooperation; they interrupt political and economic contacts; they interfere with cultural and scientific exchange; they dissolve sporting and tourist connections (in other words, the grain embargo, the Olympic boycott, the scientific boycott, etc., responses to the invasion of Afghanistan and the persecution of scientists in the USSR).

This theme was taken up by most of the speakers with only minor variations. The main speaker, Comrade Ponomarev, suggested a whole program of action intended to bring America's aggressive circles into compliance. He appealed for unity among all those concerned with preservation of peace, irrespective of their political views. "The time has come for action, not words," he said. (Wait a minute, have we not met this sentiment somewhere already? Surely not in the CND official booklet?)

The show proceeded smoothly, exhibiting the whole gallery of monsters, from the greatest peace-lover of our time, Yasir Arafat, to a "representative" of Afghanistan.

How did all these 2,260 representatives of Social Democrats, trade unions, youth, women, and religious organizations react? Did they rush out in disgust? Did they demand the withdrawal of the Soviet troops from Afghanistan in order to remove the main obstacle to détente? Did they express concern about the massive Soviet arms build-up and the deployment of SS-20s? By no means. This self-appointed World Parliament issued an Appeal in which the main ideas of Comrade Ponomarev's speech were repeated. Thus, the "Parliament" is opposed "to the vast machine and arms build-up of the most aggressive forces of imperialism which seek to take the world toward a nuclear abyss; to the falsehoods and lies of the propaganda in favor of the arms build-up, which are disseminated through imperialist-controlled mass media."

Translated from party jargon, this constitutes a clear directive to work against the armament programs of the Western countries (first of all, of course, the U.S.—the "most aggressive forces of imperialism"), and to reject any "lies" of the mass media about the Soviet arms build-up.

Beyond this, the "parliamentarians" set "the new tasks and duties . . . for action of the peoples of all continents" and worked out the Charter of the Peoples for Peace which was adopted unanimously (!) together with the Peoples' Program for Peace for the 1980s. The year 1981 was chosen to be "the springboard of the 80s, a year of a decisive offensive of the peace forces to achieve a breakthrough in curbing the arms build-up."

Most of the program was carried out, the mass demonstrations of October 1981 in the European capitals having been planned within a framework of what is called in the Soviet program "UN Disarmament Week (October 24–31)." How on earth could the Soviets have known in 1980 about events that would take place at the end of 1981, unless they were running the whole show?

My pointing out this strange coincidence, which I did in an article in the London *Times* (December 4, 1981), was bound to provoke heated denials; and did so. The Soviets in *Literaturnaya Gazetta* (December 23, 1981), as well as the CND leaders in the London *Times* (December 9, 1981), made much of the fact that UN Disarmament Week had originally been designated as an annual observance by the UN General Assembly as early as June 1978. Now, the UN flag may seem to many to be a perfect cover. One must ask, however, why virtually nothing happened during that all-important week in 1978 or 1979—even the Sofia meeting was scheduled in September, not October, of 1980—until details for its observance were specified by the Soviet-inspired program? Moreover, if one looks through the *Final Document of the Assembly Session on Disarmament (May 23-July 1, 1978)*, issued by the UN, one can find hundreds of designated weeks, months, years, and decades, all totally ignored by our peace-lovers, whereas the suggestion singled out by the Soviets was the one, the *only* one, to gather thousands in the streets. For example, was anyone aware that the decade 1969 to 1979 was solemnly declared by the United Nations to be "The Decade of Disarmament"? If there were any huge rallies or vigorous campaigns during these ten years, they seem to have escaped notice.

But let us return to this remarkable program, unanimously adopted by the international community of peace-lovers. (It is published by the World Peace Council in Helsinki, as already noted, and is available in English under the title, *Program of Action 1981*.)

This program includes such items as the "elimination of all artificial barriers to world trade," an amazingly frank recognition of the Soviet need for Western goods and technology and its desire to be granted the status of most favored nation. But what this has to do with the problem of peace and why all peace-loving people should fight for it tooth and nail is hardly made clear.

As could be expected, the program contains a clear definition of "just" and "unjust" wars: "The policy of destabilization of *progressive regimes* in developing countries actually constitutes an aggression, waged by psychological, economic, political, and other means, including armed intervention." However, similar acts against "racist and Fascist" regimes are quite justified because the mere

65

existence of nonprogressive regimes "is abhorrent to the conscience of humankind." Accordingly, the sale of arms to these "abhorrent" countries should be banned, but nothing need restrain the peace-loving from selling arms to "progressive" regimes and to "liberation movements."

And, of course, there are directives to the mass media, which "must serve the cause of peace and not the military-industrial complex by confusing public opinion with lies and disinformation." (In other words, the media should not report on the Soviet arms build-up.) A similar directive is issued to those "who bear responsibility for educating a new generation."

The program further specifies precisely which events and campaigns to undertake, and designates weeks for the collection of signatures on various petitions, etc., all around the world. It constantly emphasizes the urgent need for "further intensification of actions against the deployment of the new U.S. weapons of mass annihilation in Western Europe" and plans for "strengthening and broadening of national movements into a worldwide network of peace organizations."

It is not possible here to discuss all the details of this remarkable document. It simply introduces each and every aspect of Soviet foreign policy wrapped around with the phraseology of peace. Not surprisingly, therefore, it includes Afghanistan under the guise of a "week of solidarity, with special emphasis on support for a political settlement as proposed by the Afghan government." For Ethiopia it proposes "a week of solidarity with the Ethiopian revolution" and "support for the struggle of the Ethiopian people against imperialist and reactionary conspiracies and plans in the Horn of Africa." For Kampuchea there should be an "international campaign of solidarity with the government and people of Kampuchea led by the National United Front for National Salvation and an international campaign for recognition of the People's Revolutionary Council of Kampuchea and the seating of its representatives in the UN; exposure of the conspiracies of the Peking hegemonists who are working in collusion with the U.S. imperialists against Kampuchea." For Israel: "Support for the peace forces in Israel in their struggle for the complete withdrawal of Israel from the occupied territories and for the realization of the inalienable national rights of the Palestinian people." Whereas for the Middle East in general: a "campaign of solidarity with the Arab peoples in their struggle to liquidate the political and military consequences of the Camp David and Washington accords; solidarity actions with Libya against the threats of aggression by the Egyptian regime and U.S. imperialism." As for the U.S., even in so totally pro-Soviet a document as this the instruction to campaign for the "release of political prisoners in the United States of America" reads like a bad joke. Clearly, the love of peace dulls the sense of humor. The only countries where violations of human rights are recognized by the unanimous vote of 2,260 delegates from 137 countries are: Bolivia, Chile, El Salvador, Guatemala, Haiti, Israel, Paraguay, Uruguay, Indonesia, South Korea, Northern Ireland, and the U.S. Has the world not undergone a remarkable improvement?

After the successful adoption of this program, what followed was simple. Returning from Sofia, the enthusiastic delegates threw themselves into a hectic round of implementing the program, pressing for appropriate resolutions, actions, and commitments in each of their respective organizations (*Pravda*, November 5, 1980). An additional impetus was given to the campaign by an endorsement from the World Council of Churches at their meeting in Dresden (East Germany) on August 28, 1981, thus committing a huge number of adherents of the various Christian denominations to following the Soviet line. And in no time hundreds of thousands in the West came honestly to believe that they were out to save world peace.

Well, is there any further need to explain why the Soviet Union is so interested in the peace movement? There is a term in party jargon coined by Lenin himself: "a useful idiot." Now, in spite of all their blunders, senseless adventures, economic disasters, the Polish crisis and the stubborn resistance of the Afghan peasants, Reagan's rearmament plan and UN resolutions, the Soviet rulers have scored a spectacular victory: they have recruited millions of useful idiots to implement their bankrupt foreign policy. They are no longer isolated and there is still a big question as to whether the Americans will be allowed to place missiles in Europe.

True enough, the American economy is vastly more productive and efficient than the Soviet, but the Americans don't have a weapon like the "struggle for peace." True again, this peace movement will be expensive for the Soviet people (the meeting in Bulgaria alone must have cost them millions, to say nothing of subsidizing all peace activists on those jaunts to the best Soviet resorts; the cost of running this worldwide campaign must be simply astronomical). Still, it is cheaper than another round of the arms race, let alone the cost of maintaining a priceless military superiority. And the result will be long-lasting.

Mind you, we are into only the second year of a planned ten-year "struggle for peace." Within a few years, the whole earth will be trembling under the marching feet of the useful idiots, for their resources are inexhaustible.

I remember in the 1950s, when the previous peace campaign was still in full swing, there was a popular joke which people in the Soviet Union whispered to each other: "A Jew came to his rabbi and asked: 'Rabbi, you are a very wise man. Tell me, is there going to be a war?' 'There will be no war,' replied the rabbi, 'but there will be such a struggle for peace that no stone will be left standing.'"

II

One of the most serious mistakes of the Western peace movement and of its ideologists is the obdurate refusal to understand the nature of the Soviet regime, and the concomitant effort to lift the question of peace out of the context of the broader problem of East-West relations. After several decades of listening to what they believe to be "anti-Communist propaganda," they have simply got "fed-up with it." They ascribe everything they hear about the East to a "cold-war-type brainwashing," and make no attempt to distinguish what is true from what is not. This attitude, which I can only describe as a combination of ignorance and arrogance, makes them an easy target for any pseudo-theory (or outright Soviet propaganda) that happens to be fashionable at any given moment. Besides, baffled by endless and contradictory arguments among the "specialists" about the nature of the Soviet system, the leaders of the peace movement believe they have found a "new approach" which makes the entire problem irrelevant.

A few months ago in England, I attended a public debate on the problem of unilateral disarmament. The leader of a big peace group opened his speech by saying that from his standpoint, it is irrelevant who is the aggressor and who the victim. He said: "It is like when two boys have a fight in the churchyard. It is impossible to find out who started the fight, nor is there any need to do so. What we should do is to stop them."

This metaphor reflects very well the prevailing attitude among peace-movement members. They believe they have gotten around a baffling problem, whereas they have in fact inadvertently adopted the concept of the "normal opponent." From the "churchyard" standpoint, the present conflict seems very ordinary: two bullies have become so embittered by their prolonged quarrel—in which anyway the essence of the disagreement has been lost or forgotten—that they are quite prepared to kill each other and everybody else around. They are temporarily insane, mad, but are basically normal human beings. Pride and fury will not permit them to come to their senses, unless we, the sane people around them, are prepared to intervene. Let us make them talk to one another, let us pin down their hands, let us distract them from their quarrel. We cannot, to be sure, pin down the hands of one of them. Then, in the best Christian tradition, let us make the other repent, in all good Christian humility. Let us disarm him to convince his adversary of his peaceful intentions. Let us turn the other cheek. Sooner or later the other will come to feel ashamed.

This view sums up exactly what I mean by a combination of ignorance and arrogance. Indeed, if we look upon the world from the "churchyard" standpoint, there probably is no need to find out who is the aggressor and who the victim. There is no need for police or armed forces. All we can see is a row of graves with the dead lying orderly in them and a couple of children quarreling with each other. Unfortunately, outside the church walls there is a bigger and far more dangerous world with gangsters, murderers, rapists, and other perverse characters.

Needless to say, this churchyard model simply does not

merit serious consideration. Unfortunately, it is a widespread belief (and not only within the peace movement) that the Soviet government, like any other government, is preoccupied with the well-being of its people, and will therefore be eager to reduce military expenditures. This notion comes so naturally to our peacemakers that they just do not notice they have taken on a view of the Soviet system which is both very old and unquestionably wrong. If they only took the trouble to study a little Soviet history, they would know immediately how misleading this seemingly natural view is. Not only are the Soviet rulers indifferent to the living condition of their populace, they *deliberately* keep it low; on the other hand, disarmament (irrespective of the problem of well-being) would lead very rapidly to the collapse of the Soviet empire.

Normally we try to understand an opponent by taking his place, getting into his shoes, so to speak. That is why most people try to explain Soviet behavior in terms of "normal human motives," that is, by motives familiar to them. And that is exactly why they constantly pile one mistake upon another. For it is extremely difficult for a "normal" human being to put himself inside the skin of a mentally ill one. It is almost as in nature itself: when we test natural phenomena under extreme conditions, we suddenly find some unpredictable anomaly that is baffling to us. Logic itself becomes abnormal in certain extreme cases. If we add up two numbers, say, or multiply or divide them, we invariably obtain a new number. But if we use zero or infinity our whole rule suddenly goes wrong.

But let us take an example relevant to the present discussion. Let us take the key question: why is the Soviet Union so aggressive, so eager to expand? We see how many schools of thought there are among those studying the problem (and we see, too, how all of them are wrong).

There are some people who believe that the present Soviet expansionism is just a continuation of the Russian prerevolutionary colonial policy. In other words, it is a bad legacy. Indeed, this notion about Soviet expansionism was the dominant one for a very long time—and still is in some quarters. In line with it, there have been repeated attempts to offer the Soviets a division of the world into spheres of influence. We owe to it the Yalta agreement, the Potsdam agreement, and assorted other disasters. Each time the Soviets have accepted the division into spheres of influence, and each time they have violated it. Is this because they need more mineral resources, more territory, a wider market for their goods? No. Their own territory is undeveloped, their own mineral resources are in the earth, they do not have enough goods for their own internal market. There are no useful mineral deposits in Cuba or Afghanistan. There is no Russian national interest in Angola or Vietnam. In fact, these new "colonies" cost the Soviet people many millions of dollars a day apiece. So, Soviet policy is no classical case of colonialism.

Then there is another theory, far more pernicious because much more widely accepted and because to reject it one needs a real knowledge of Soviet life. I mean the theory according to which Soviet aggressiveness is the result of the fear of hostile encirclement. The proponents of this theory argue that Russian history, particularly the history of repeated invasions of Russian territory within the last century, has made the Russian people almost paranoid about an external threat.

This theory sounds very scientific because many facts may be cited to back it up. Still, it is no more than a shrewd combination of obvious lies, wrong interpretations, and very perfunctory knowledge. It is mainly based on an overestimation of the importance of history for any given nation and on an oversimplification of the Soviet system.

To begin with, there is an obvious lie in this theory—that is, a deliberate confusion between the people and the government in the USSR. Those who know the Soviet system only moderately well may still need to be reminded that the people have no privilege of representation in the government—that is, have no free elections. Thus, the government does not reflect the feelings of the population. So if we are to believe that the population is frightened by the long history of invasions, the government has no reason to share these fears. The Soviet government, with its vast and omnipresent intelligence system, is extremely well-informed about every move and every smallest intention of the West (anyway not very difficult to achieve in view of the remarkable openness of Western societies). By 1978–79, when their arms build-up was at a high pitch, whom were they supposed to be so afraid of? Their great friend, the French President Giscard? Or their even better friend in West Germany, Willy Brandt? Britain, with its puny armed forces (and ongoing discussion on unilateral disarmament), or perhaps Nixon and Carter, who between them shelved all the major armament programs? Japan, which has no army at all?

Clearly the Soviet government had no reason to be frightened. In fact, the theory of Soviet paranoia does not imply a frightened government, but rather a frightened *nation*. In a "normal" country this might drive the government to become aggressive. But in the Soviet Union the people mean nothing and have no way of pressuring their government to do anything. They would not be allowed to voice any fears. So, who is so frightened in the Soviet Union? Besides, as far as the rulers are concerned, their own experience of war, World War II, could not frighten them for a very simple reason: they won the war. Can you show me any victorious general who is so afraid of war as to become paranoid? The psychology of Soviet rulers is in any case totally different.

One need only look at a map of the world to see how ridiculous this theory is. Can we honestly believe that the poor Communists in the Kremlin are so frightened that they must protect themselves by sending their troops to Cuba and Cuban troops to Angola? By sending military equipment and advisers to Ethiopia and Vietnam and then by sending Vietnamese troops to Kampuchea? Take another look at that map: it is not at all obvious that the USSR is encircled by hostile powers. Rather the other way around: it is the Western world that is encircled by the hostile hordes of the Communists. Well, if their paranoia can be satisfied only by surrendering the whole world to their control, what difference can it make to us whether they act out of fear or out of endemic aggressiveness?

Finally, and most importantly for an understanding of this pernicious theory, is the fact that it was invented by the Kremlin propaganda experts. It was very successfully exploited in the years of détente, when Western governments, acting under its influence, deliberately permitted the Soviets to achieve military superiority. They would probably deny it now, but I remember very well the discussions of that period. The argument of the ideologists of détente was that once the Soviets caught up, they would relax; this would in turn lead to the internal as well as external relaxation of the Communist regime, i.e., to *liberalization*. The results of this brilliant experiment we can see now.

The Soviet population, too, has been subjected, day after day for sixty-five years, to an intense propaganda campaign about this putative "hostile encirclement." The Communist rulers unscrupulously exploit the tragedy of the Soviet people in World War II for the purpose of justifying both their oppressive regime and their monstrous military spending. They try their best to instill into the people a pathological fear of the "capitalist world." Fortunately, the people are sane enough to laugh at the very idea. Thus, contrary to this theory, there is no paranoid population demanding to be protected in the Soviet Union, despite the best efforts of a perfectly sober and cruel government.

No, it is not the fear of invasion or a World War II hangover that has driven the Soviet rulers to wage an undeclared war against the whole world for half a century now. It is their commitment—repeated quite openly every five years at each Party Congress since the beginning of this century—to support the "forces of progress and socialism," to support "liberation movements," everywhere on the globe.

Are we then to assume that the Soviet leadership consists of fanatics aiming at global control? Even such a model, crazy as it might sound, still imputes too much "normality" to the Soviet leaders. Or, more precisely, it is too big a simplification. This theory, too—fortunately for us—does not fit a number of the facts. Paradoxically, none of the present Communist leaders believes any longer in Communist doctrine. Fortunately, because no real fanatic would ever tolerate the destruction of the object of his obsession. He would rather witness the destruction of the entire world.

The Soviet rulers are a totally cynical lot, much more preoccupied with their own privileges and pleasures than with Marxist ideas. They probably hate Communist dogma more than any Western capitalist. Moreover, the majority of the Soviet people are as cynical as their leaders. There are many more sincere Communists to be found in the West than in the USSR.

But this fact has also created false hopes among Western politicians and the public. The same false hopes encouraged by the theory of encirclement—that it will be possible to treat the Soviets as normal partners at last, that it will be possible to negotiate, to cooperate, and to relax. Both theories lead equally to the same mistaken policy.

So what is the truth about the damned Soviet system?

Certainly, there was a period when the Soviet leaders were Communist fanatics, ready to sacrifice the whole world to their faith. There was a period, too, when at least some part of the population was prepared to greet this new idea with considerable enthusiasm. The people of my country, I suppose, could be excused for their delusion, because communism was indeed a new idea and one that might be thought by the inexperienced to appeal to the best qualities in human nature. Is it after all not a worthy purpose, to secure unalloyed happiness for all future generations, to liberate and unite the whole of mankind? Naturally, such a thing will not be easy, but it is worth a great deal of sacrifice to achieve. Just as naturally there will be many selfish people to oppose it and we should learn to be ruthless with them. Only millions of individual wills fused into a single invincible "we," united by the iron fist of a leader, can achieve so difficult an end.

This period of ecstasy, however, was very short-lived. One by one, the various elements of the Soviet population cooled down, sobered up, and then could not believe in their own former enthusiasm. The besieged minority reacted to this desertion of the public by becoming even more ruthless and single-minded: "We will make them happy against their will; their children will be grateful to us." I will not describe the mass slaughter that resulted from this great determination. It has been described many times. A terrorized majority obeyed with sham enthusiasm, because it was a crime to look gloomy. But underneath there was a silent, passive resistance. The minority of "believers" over time became simply a ruling clique which had lost its ideals in the constant fight for survival, in corruption, and in its abuses of power and its privileges. The ensuing political situation can best be described as a latent civil war in which a kind of balance has been maintained by political terror.

In this way the Soviet Union reached a condition in which absolute power was exercised by absolutely cynical people over absolutely cynical people, each side vociferously assuring the other that they were all still sincerely building an ideal future society. But the ideology exists now almost as in a work of science fiction: it has separated itself from its substratum and has petrified in the structure of the society. It has become an institution in which nobody (not even the top executive) is allowed verbally to deviate from the dead dogma. The will of millions is still being taken from them and welded into the iron fist of abstraction.

There is practically no free human being inside the entire country. The state—the only employer—will not allow anyone to be financially independent—as indeed no independence of any kind will be tolerated. Everybody must be carrying out a useful task, performing a needed function. Several nationwide networks of security and secret police spy first on each other and then together on everybody else. Such a system has created a new type of a man, who thinks one thing, publicly expresses another, and does a third.

The enormous inertia of this system is not surprising. There is no internal "class enemy" any more; there is no need to terrorize so many millions. Still, there are huge concentration camps, because they have become an integral part of the country's economic, political, and spiritual life. Nobody believes now in the ultimate victory of communism in the world, but the policy of external subversion and the promotion of "socialist forces" everywhere has become an integral part of the state machinery. The system rules the people.

Beyond inertia, there is something else, something even more decisive: the instinct of self-preservation of the ruling clique. Once you are riding a tiger, it is difficult to jump off. Any attempt at internal liberalization might prove fatal. If the central power were to weaken, the sheer amount of hatred accumulated within the population for these sixty-five years of the Socialist experiment would be so dangerous, the results of any reform so unpredictable—and, above all, the power, the fabulous privileges, the very physical survival of the ruling clique would become so tenuous—that one would be mad to expect the Soviet leaders to play with liberal ideas. Only the imminent threat of total collapse might force them to introduce internal reforms.

The two sides of the Soviet regime—internal oppression and external aggression—are inseparably interlocked, creating a sort of vicious circle. The more the regime becomes rotten inside, the more pains are taken by its leaders to present a formidable façade to the outside world. They need international tension as a thief needs the darkness of the night. In the political climate of latent civil war, given the enormous and senseless sacrifices of the last fifty years, the constant economic difficulties, and the lack of basic rights—not to mention, again, the extraordinary privileges enjoyed by the ruling clique—the only hope for stability lies in the need to cope with an external threat: "hostile encirclement" and the subversive activity of "world imperialism." In this artificially created state of war, the worker's demand for a better deal, or a captive nation's demand for its independence, can then be treated as an act of subversion, "playing into the hands of the enemy."

Nor is it enough to create a devil in order to maintain one's religious zeal. This imaginary enemy must be defeated over and over again or there will be the risk that he will seduce you. American "imperialism" must be defeated at any cost, and the liberation of proletarians in the capitalist countries must be promoted by all means. The failure to support a "friendly government," to establish Communist rule in a new country, will immediately be perceived as a weakening of Soviet power, and therefore an encouragement to the sullen and embittered population at home. Any failure of the Soviet international adventure may thus trigger a chain reaction leading to the ultimate collapse of the Soviet rulers. This is why they cannot allow a popular uprising in Hungary, a "Prague Spring" in Czechoslovakia, an anti-Communist "Holy War" in Afghanistan, or an independent alternative center of power in Poland. Immediate repercussions would be felt in all the other countries of the Socialist camp as well as in the Ukraine, the Baltic states, Central Asia, and other occupied territories. The scenario of aggression is depressingly uniform. First, the Soviets undermine a democratic state, helping the friendly "progressive forces" come to power. Next, they have to save their bankrupt "progressive" friends, when the resistance of the population threatens to overthrow them.

Are they frightened to the point of aggressiveness? Yes,

but not by your piles of hardware, not by your clumsy attempts at defense. They are frightened by their own people, because they know the end is inevitable. That is why they must score victory after victory over the "hostile encirclement." Behind every victory is a very simple message addressed to their own enslaved population: "Look, we are still very strong and nobody dares to challenge our might."

If they are afraid of you, it is because they are afraid of your freedom and your prosperity. They cannot tolerate a democratic state close to their borders (and then, close to the borders of their buffer-states), because a bad example of thriving democracy so close at hand might prove to be too provocative.

Knowing all this, let us ask ourselves a question: what would happen if the West were to disarm unilaterally? Could the Soviets follow suit? Certainly not. It would mean the rapid disintegration of their empire and a general collapse of their power. Does this mean they will simply roll over the now defenseless Western countries? Again, the answer is no. They don't need your territory, which would be difficult to hold anyway. Above all, where would they acquire goods, technology, credits, grain, etc., if they were to impose on you their inefficient economic system? They need you in the way China needs Hong Kong. *But from that very moment you will gradually begin to lose your freedom, being exposed to constant and unrestrained Soviet blackmail.*

You may like or dislike your trade unions, but would you like them to have to consider a possibility of foreign invasion every time they wanted to declare a strike—as Solidarity had to do in Poland for eighteen months? You may like or dislike your mass media, but would you like to see the self-censorship of your press in order to avoid an angry reaction by a powerful neighbor—as in Finland? You may like or dislike your system of representation, but at least you are free to elect those whom you choose without considering the desires of a foreign power. Nobody threatens to come into your country and impose a government of its choosing—as in Afghanistan. The nature of the Soviet system is such that it can never be satisfied until you are similar to them and are totally under their control.

So, we come to a very important conclusion: the issue now is not "peace versus war," but rather "freedom versus slavery." Peace and freedom appear to be inseparable, and the old formula "Better red than dead" is simply fatuous. Those who live by it will be both red *and* dead. Whether we like it or not, there will be no peace in our world, no relaxation of international tension, no fruitful cooperation between East and West, until the Soviet internal system changes drastically.

Has this simple and self-evident truth ever been understood by Western decision makers? I doubt it. In a way, I can share some of the concern of the peace movement. Because for the West to react stereotypically by increasing military spending and stockpiling new hardware every time the Soviet instability-aggression complex manifests itself is simply to miss the target. At any rate, it is not enough. It is not going to change the Soviet system. It is not going to prevent Soviet expansion, especially in the Third World. Soviet ideological warfare is far shrewder than a big nuclear bludgeon. Would we, for instance, consider a nuclear bombardment if tomorrow there were to be a revolt of various tribes in Pakistan, instigated by Moscow? Or a Communist takeover in Iran?

There are plenty of "natural" troubles in the world, brought on by local conditions. But the influence of Moscow immediately turns them into major strategic problems. It would be senseless to try to solve all such problems by military means all over the globe. Simple logic suggests that we must deal first of all with the *source* of the world's major trouble—i.e., the Soviet system. We must find an effective way to help the Soviet population in its struggle for change. After all, they are our biggest ally.

Unfortunately, this has so far never been appreciated by the West, which has instead been continuously strengthening the Soviet system by credits, trade, technology. Why should the Soviets bother to introduce any internal reforms if their inefficient economy is periodically saved by the West? The West is still rich enough to help them out, and Siberia is also rich enough in turn to sell natural gas, gold, diamonds.

We may shake with indignation whenever we hear about the Soviet invasion of yet another country. We hate these little obedient soldiers, ever ready to do whatever they are told. Are they robots? But what do we propose that they should do? Do we honestly expect them to rebel and face a firing squad, while the entire world continues to provide their executioners with goods, credits, and modern technology? Don't we demand of them much more than we demand of ourselves? Somewhere, somehow, this vicious circle must be broken, if we are to survive as human beings. Why not start where it is easier?

There are 90,000 of these "robots" trapped in Afghanistan at this very moment. They cannot rebel because they will be shot down. Even so, there are occasional rebellions (and executions). They cannot desert, because they will either be killed in the process or, if they are lucky and manage to reach Pakistan, the Pakistani authorities will return them to the Soviet command (that is, again, to the firing squad). Does any government try to help them? No. Instead, several European governments have decided to buy Soviet natural gas, perhaps the very same gas that is being pumped out of Afghanistan by the Soviet occupation authorities as compensation for "liberating" Afghanistan.

There is a lot of noise about Poland right now. A lot of noise, and a lot of smoke screens. But does any government sacrifice anything? After issuing thunderous condemnations, the European governments decided not to apply economic sanctions against the Eastern bloc, because sanctions would "harm us, probably, more than them." Why should you establish the kind of relations that only make you more vulnerable than the enemy? Why do you continue to sign new agreements of the same type (natural gas, for example)? The American banks recently decided to cover the huge Polish deficit because the "bankruptcy of Poland would undermine the world financial system." What would happen, I wonder, if tomorrow the Soviet-bloc countries were to refuse to pay their debts and to suspend all trade?

This is what the struggle for peace and freedom boils down to: the people in the East should sacrifice their lives, but you should not sacrifice your profits. Small wonder that the Polish army does not rebel.

In fact, the imposition of economic sanctions on the Polish military junta and on their Soviet masters is not just a possible step; it is the actual *obligation* of the Western countries under the terms of the Helsinki agreement. A direct link among security, economic cooperation, and the observance of human rights is the very essence of this agreement. If that is forgotten now, of what point is all the noise lately heard from Madrid?

To tell the truth, I do not believe that any of it has been forgotten. Neither do I believe that the Western banks,

83

industrialists, and governments are so "stupid" as to tie themselves to the Eastern chariot wheels by mistake. It is their deliberate policy, overtly articulated in the time of détente, and covertly now. Moreover, it is their philosophy. They love stability, these bankers and businessmen. And they are much against any resistance movement in the Communist countries, very much against any prospect of liberation for the enslaved nations of the East. They are the greatest peace-lovers of all, far more powerful than all those crowds on the streets of the European capitals. Thanks to them, we descend slowly into the Age of Darkness.

III

This article is not addressed to the bankers, or to the governments. I do not expect any help from them. In spite of all the harsh words used in it, I wish it to be read by sincere people who are seriously concerned with the problems of peace and freedom. They will probably dislike many of the things I have said here. I hope, however, that they will understand its main point: that peace has never been preserved by a hysterical desire to survive at any price. Nor has it ever been promoted by catchy phrases and cheap slogans. There are 400 million people in the East whose freedom was stolen from them and whose existence is miserable. It so happens that peace is impossible while they remain enslaved, and only with them (not with their executioners) should you work to secure real peace in our world.

Your recent mass demonstrations were disastrous, because in them you identified yourselves, willingly or unwillingly, with the rulers of the Eastern countries. To make broad alliances with any public (or governmental) forces just for the sake of power is a tremendous mistake. This mistake must be corrected if we are to live in peace and freedom. We should know who are our friends and who are our enemies. The fate of Solidarity should open our eyes.

---

1. Much of the material that follows here on the early days of World War II is taken from the book by Nikolai Tolstoy, *Stalin's Secret War* (1981), where the appropriate references can be found.

2. The European peace movement split in 1982–83, after this article was written, and now several groups or spokespersons (e.g., CND, Professor E. P. Thompson, and groups within the Green movement) have become outspokenly critical of Soviet behavior in Poland and Afghanistan, and of Soviet treatment of dissidents.—V.B.

The Catholic Bishops'
Search for Peace

by James Hitchcock

JAMES HITCHCOCK *is professor of history at St. Louis University and is a prolific writer on religious and cultural subjects. He has written several well-known books, including* The Decline and Fall of Radical Catholicism *and* Catholicism and Modernity. *His latest book,* What Is Secular Humanism?, *has become a best seller. A Roman Catholic layman, Professor Hitchcock is best known for his able defense of orthodox Christianity and his piercing analysis of modern secular humanism.*

Perhaps no statement ever issued by the Catholic bishops of the United States has attracted more attention, much of it excited and even fevered, than their 1983 pastoral letter on war and peace, *The Challenge of Peace: God's Promise and Our Response.*[1] The letter was debated for nearly two years before being issued in the spring of 1983; never has an episcopal document been subjected to such intense scrutiny by so many people for so long. By the time of its final adoption (by a vote of 238 to 9), scarcely a phrase in the letter had escaped the closest analysis.

But even the most prolonged debate was not sufficient to dispel all doubts and disagreements. By their own admission the bishops were venturing into unfamiliar territory, into a subject about which the American people (as well as much of the Western world) are deeply divided. The bishops' willingness to issue such a provocative letter indicates a certain courage. However, from another standpoint, it also manifests a lack of that same virtue.

The letter is lengthy and detailed—32 pages of triple-columned fine print, with 127 footnotes. This alone makes it unlikely that more than a relatively few people will read it carefully, even among the priests and nuns charged with conveying its substance to their people. Like many public documents, there is something in it for everyone, and different people will quote the passages which best conform to their own moral and political predilections. In the end the document may be less important for what it actually says than for what people think it says, and for its overall symbolic significance.

On one level the document affirms principles that scarcely any Catholic could legitimately question, and it does so with reference to the traditional doctrine of the "just war," a theory which has dominated Catholic thinking on the subject since the time of St. Augustine (ca. A.D. 400).

Not only is a national right of self-defense reaffirmed, but also a national duty, recalling the words of Pope Pius XII in 1948: "A people threatened with an unjust aggression, or already its victim, may not remain passively indifferent, if it would think and act as befits a Christian." Classical Catholic political thought defines the defense of its citizens as one of the principal reasons for the existence of the state.

The bishops then recall the classical criteria of a just war—that it be fought for a just cause, that it be proclaimed by legitimate public authority, that the warring nation have a preponderance of justice on its side, that it have the intention to right injustice, that war be a last resort, that there be a probability of success, and that there be a proportion of means to ends in the prosecution of the war.

This leads to the issue of *jus in bello*—law in war—moral limits within which war must be fought if all other criteria are satisfied. Here American bishops raise the issue of nuclear warfare and sketch out a position which is "profoundly skeptical" of its legitimacy. For, they argue, nuclear weaponry has in effect changed the nature of war itself, making it extremely doubtful if there can be a proper proportion of means to end. Modern nuclear war is likely to be "unwinnable," and it will prove impossible to distinguish properly military targets from civilian targets which, according to the just-war theory, must be spared.

The document therefore forbids "counter-population warfare," as well as the initiation of nuclear war, and expresses profound doubts about the possibility of limited nuclear war. Thus it questions the legitimacy of nuclear weapons in and of themselves.

At this point the bishops make a somewhat grudging concession to the doctrine of deterrence, which has been at the heart of the American defense system since 1945—the idea that it is permissible, and indeed necessary, to maintain a readiness for nuclear war in order to deter other world powers from initiating such a war. Citing an address by Pope John Paul II to the United Nations, the bishops accept the morality of deterrence, but only so long as it accompanies a sincere effort to achieve progressive disarmament.

In its evaluation of deterrence, and in certain specific policy recommendations which follow, the letter becomes controversial, as it leaves aside broad principles which are widely accepted and it enters the heart of current political controversy. The bishops forbid planning for nuclear war (since the purpose of having the weapons is merely deterrence), striving for nuclear superiority ("sufficiency" alone is justified), increasing the number of armaments, and blurring the distinction between nuclear and conventional warfare. They urge bilateral, mutually verifiable disarmament agreements, reduction of nuclear arsenals, and removal of such weapons from sensitive areas of the globe.

Meanwhile, the bishops argue, nations not only must limit armed conflict but must search for genuine peace. Efforts must be made toward "nonviolent means of conflict resolution" and a strengthening of international organizations such as the United Nations.

The final version of the letter was the beneficiary of countless interventions and arguments, to the point where it considered most aspects of the question, if only to reject some of them.

The initial draft, in spring 1982, was almost universally criticized and quickly discarded.[2] Ironically, criticisms from both liberals and conservatives converged on the same point; the document seemed to say that the possession of nuclear weapons was wrong but that such possession was nonetheless permissible. From the Left the bishops were urged to condemn even their possession, while theologically orthodox Catholics pointed out the devastating implications of condemning an action as immoral, yet still permitting it.

The second draft sought to resolve the contradiction in a quasi-pacifist direction.[3] In this draft the possession of nuclear weapons seemed to be condemned. Critics charged that it failed to respect the right of national self-defense or to take note of the realities of international politics. This second draft was enthusiastically hailed by the religious Left.

However, the third draft was substantially changed in the other direction, to the point where leftist critics charged that it had been rendered mere pious exhortation.[4] Liberal bishops organized to amend the document on the floor of the bishops' meeting, and for the most part succeeded. What was symbolically most important, setting the tone for what followed, was an amendment which changed a demand for a "curb" in the production of nuclear weapons to a "halt." To liberals, this change established a decidedly antinuclear bias in the letter.[5]

In issuing their letter, the bishops consciously sought to avoid a statement which could be regarded as merely platitudinous. If they were to speak to one of the overwhelming issues of the day, they would do so in terms which commanded attention, or so they reasoned. In the process, they also rendered themselves vulnerable to criticisms based on fact—many of their moral judgments imply assumptions about the condition of the world which may not be true, or can be a cause of legitimate disagreement.

Among their factual assumptions most frequently questioned are: that nuclear war could never be limited; that all nuclear weapons are by nature more destructive than all conventional weapons; that a reduction in nuclear arsenals would make war less likely; and that good will and effort are mainly what are needed to arrive at viable disarmament agreements. While the principles of the letter remain valid, their application stands or falls on the correctness of these factual assumptions. If the assumptions prove to be incorrect, then the letter is not "relevant" in the way the bishops intended it to be. (The letter makes a link between the nuclear-weapons issue and abortion, inviting readers to be "prolife" on both questions. But one difference between the two is that the facts of abortion are not in question—no one argues that legalized abortions deter fetuses from being killed, for example.)

The bishops themselves recognized the uncertainties of their approach and reminded their readers that not everything in the letter is of equal authority. A distinction is to be made between principles which are morally binding on all Catholics and applications which may be the subject of legitimate debate. However, the letter offers little specific guidance in distinguishing between the two. Furthermore, it has been enthusiastically hailed, by its most fervent supporters, precisely because of some of its most dubious sections, which are those directly relevant to current political debates. In practice the distinction between firm principle and debatable application is likely to be a difficult one to maintain.

In seeking to be prophetic, the bishops also chose an

unhappy method of proceeding, one which pays greater tribute to their "openness" than to their ability to wear the prophet's mantle. The letter was intensely debated at every stage, and no part of it was left immune from the most exacting public scrutiny. When certain sections (even the entire first draft) aroused too much negative comment, they were scrapped, or were revised radically. Deep disagreements within the episcopal house were revealed to the whole world. Many people praised this procedure as a sign of a growingly democratic church. But a group of bishops seeking to arrive at truth through public debate and democratic consensus can scarcely claim, at the same time, to be prophetic. It was as if the Supreme Court were to issue provisional opinions on its cases, which it would then rescind and reissue in the face of public criticism.

The bishops did not give the impression of being firmly in command of either the principles or the applications, a fact which was evident from the beginning. Thus one of their chosen advisors was a priest-theologian, Charles Curran, who for years has been a vocal and active public dissenter from official Catholic teaching on sexual morality.[6] That he was chosen to advise the bishops on war and peace suggested that they did not rate fidelity to the Catholic moral tradition high on their list of essential criteria.

Theologically conservative commentators (not necessarily those who disagreed with the letter's specific conclusions) sharply criticized both the first and second drafts for their use of "consequentialism" (the moral philosophy which judges human acts primarily by their likely practical effects) and "proportionalism" (which permits immoral acts if their good effects seem likely to outweigh the evil of the acts themselves). If such moral arguments had appeared in the final authoritative version of the document, the

94

American bishops would have been officially on record as accepting moral positions which would have had devastating consequences for many other areas of morality.[7] (Proportionalism and consequentialism were largely expunged from the final version, thereby leaving unresolved the question whether the possession of nuclear weapons is or is not immoral in itself.)

In its penultimate draft, the letter stated that the Second Vatican Council of 1962–65 (the most authoritative and important Catholic assembly of modern times) "endorsed" the principle of conscientious objection. That assertion was omitted from the final version, following criticism that the Council did no such thing, but merely urged governments to make humane provisions for conscientious objectors who are willing to accept alternative service.[8]

However, the letter sets up two parallel "traditions" in the Catholic church—one that of the just war, the other that of Christian pacifism—and treats them as though they are equivalent. This procedure can only be called wishful on the part of the sizable pacifist underground in the contemporary Catholic church (which includes a few bishops). For the letter itself admits that the theory of the just war has "held the field" for 1500 years. In seeking a tradition of pacifism it cites as examples one Hindu (Gandhi) and one Protestant (Martin Luther King Jr.), without discussing the ambiguities of "nonviolence" as practiced by the Indian independence movement or the civil rights movement in the United States. It also cites one contemporary Catholic—Dorothy Day of the Catholic Worker movement, although her position was defined precisely by its divergence from the mainstream of Catholic thinking. In the history of the church, outside the earliest centuries, its only significant example of a pacifist is Saint Francis of Assisi, whose absolute idealism, in matters

95

of property as well as war, was never normative for the church. In fact, there is only a slender and eccentric tradition of Catholic pacifism, but the pastoral letter in effect seeks to create one full-blown.

The letter ascribes the noblest motives to pacifists and conscientious objectors, which is one way of resolving the apparent contradiction whereby both those who fight to defend their country and those who refuse are somehow serving the same end. The letter mentions almost nothing about the kinds of alternative service which pacifists might appropriately undertake.

In places the letter manifests the confusion to which the Christian in politics is easily prone—equating the ideal with the real. Not only are the difficulties created by a popular pacifism passed over in silence, the bishops seem to find nothing but a prospect for good in such ventures as the proposed "peace academy" in the United States or, especially, the United Nations. (They quote Paul VI and John Paul II on the importance of the latter body, without seeming to notice that the papal remarks contain implicit rebukes of the organization's failure to adhere to its own stated principles.)[9] While their evaluation of the possibility of nuclear war leads them to a professedly skeptical mode of reasoning about concrete realities, fashionable liberal shibboleths are supported merely on the basis of high-sounding rhetoric.

These weaknesses in the document, although somewhat secondary to its central message, reveal that its drafters were not fully cognizant of the whole Catholic theological tradition. Thus it is no surprise that the decided improvements between the second and third drafts of the letter seem to have been inspired by the Vatican itself.

Early in 1983 a delegation of American bishops met in

Rome with a delegation of West European bishops and prominent Vatican officials. Although, as is customary with high-level diplomatic conferences, official statements announced complete harmony among the participants, in fact some of the Europeans are known to have pressed the Americans to give unambiguous support to the doctrine of deterrence and to acknowledge forthrightly the reality of the Soviet threat. Vatican officials, notably Cardinal Josef Ratzinger, one of the pope's most trusted advisors, are known to have told the Americans that they should be more concerned with enunciating principles and not press their application too closely.[10] All this was reflected in the final draft, especially in numerous citations of Pope John Paul's statements, particularly his endorsement of the idea of deterrence.

A hint of the attitude of some European bishops was given when the West German hierarchy issued their own pastoral letter just a few weeks before the American bishops voted on their final version. The Germans firmly upheld the idea of deterrence, did not condemn "first use" of nuclear weapons, and seemed to hold open the possibility of their limited use.[11] Even earlier the secretary of the French council of bishops praised the Americans' third draft as a definite improvement on the second and denounced the movement toward a unilateral nuclear freeze in the West.[12] Meanwhile the Italian bishops issued a letter sharply criticizing the idea of unilateral disarmament.[13] Although the latter possibility had never been considered by the Americans, these expressions of the West Europeans' priorities seemed to be the reverse of their trans-Atlantic brethren—the Americans were preoccupied with the need for disarmament, the Europeans by the need for defense.

The second draft of the American letter was flabby in its

treatment of the Soviets. The third version, while acknowledging moral failings on the part of the United States, explicitly states that there can be no moral equation between the two powers—the Soviet system is tyrannical and destructive of human welfare, while that of the United States respects human dignity. Pockets of flabby thinking remain, however. The bishops expressly take no position concerning the origins of the Cold War, or on whether Soviet aggression is motivated mainly by defensive considerations. But they quote the pope on the fact that certain world powers are simply untrustworthy for purposes of negotiation. The pope urges that, properly cautious, other governments should negotiate anyway, advice seconded by the bishops. What is said about the Soviets seems to call into question other parts of the letter, which assume that effort and commitment alone are lacking to achieve meaningful arms agreements.

Faithful to the Catholic tradition, the bishops begin their letter by recalling that true peace is more than merely the absence of war. They also point out that there is often a tension between peace and justice, since the achievement of the latter sometimes requires the temporary sacrifice of the former. Peace is proclaimed as a positive thing.

In practice the letter makes little of this profound insight. Most of its recommendations concentrate on eliminating the possibility of war, a possibility mainly ascribed to the possession of certain weapons. Specific recommendations for the promotion of true peace drift into hazy and dubious platitudes about international cooperation. Near the end of the letter the bishops note that the world seems increasingly at odds with Christian beliefs, and they summon their people to prayer and fasting. On the whole, though, a profoundly Christian spirit does not infuse the document. Peace is understood as the absence of war, and the steps toward its achievement are not very different from those a secular humanist might urge. Specifically Christian remedies seem like afterthoughts. Above all, there is no sense that true Christian peace requires the complete moral conversion of the individual and of society, or that the state of conflict is the result of rebellion against God's order. Although some things in the letter are disconcerting to the "hawks" among the bishops' own people, little would give serious pause to nonbelievers, provided they share the letter's specific conclusions.

As suggested earlier, the circumstances surrounding the issuance of the letter are perhaps as significant as the letter itself, and it is impossible to understand its full significance without examining those circumstances.

One of the most important of these is the extraordinary enthusiasm with which it has been greeted by certain kinds of people, many of whom followed the unfolding drama of its various drafts with the avidity of baseball fanatics supporting a pennant-winning team. From the mass media, from prominent liberal politicians, and from influential pundits like the retired diplomat George Kennan, extravagant praise has been heaped on the letter. Nothing before that American bishops have said or done has called forth such encomia and such proclaimed agreement.

This is odd if, first of all, the bishops are truly being "prophetic," as is so often claimed. Surely the prophet has no right to expect lionization at the hands of some of the most powerful elements of the society, even if accompanied by criticism from others.

Odder still is the fact that the letter professes to be based on solid Catholic principles, to be a careful and authentic exposition of the Catholic doctrine of peace and war. Many of those who praise it are not Catholics, and they can hardly be supposed to have any great understanding of Catholic theology. Their reasons for hailing the document must therefore be extraneous to the document's own stated reasons. Basically, many of the enthusiasts are interested only in the "bottom line"—the specific places where the bishops "come down" on currently disputed issues. But these parts of the letter are the least certain. Furthermore, it is doubtful if the conclusions can be embraced without the reasons behind them, unless the conclusions are regarded as being essentially independent of the theological rationale which is offered for them. Thus, although the bishops aspired to be teachers and prophets, some of the very people who hailed them as such responded with disappointment and rejection when it appeared that the result of the process would be less "radical" than they desired. [14] The bishops were to be accorded the status of teachers only insofar as they said exactly what their "pupils" wanted to hear.

The most telling point is the pastoral's linking of war and abortion. It postulates a continuity of respect for life and argues that those who follow the bishops' teaching on one of these questions must follow it on the other. Whatever else it is, the passage can be regarded as a litmus test which ought to exclude those who favor the bishops' conclusions without accepting their arguments.

But from the beginning that has not been the case. Secular and religious liberals well known for their support of legalized abortion (and for their attacks on the bishops for opposing it) hailed the document enthusiastically, and scarcely entered a demurrer against the abortion passage. The National Council of Churches, the United Methodist Church, and other religious groups supporting legalized abortion endorsed the letter without difficulty. [15]

At this point it might be supposed that "prophetic"

bishops, determined not to be misunderstood, would have reentered the arena to remind their would-be allies of some of the unpalatable parts of the document. Nothing like this occurred, however. In the early summer of 1983 two of the most prominent "peace bishops"—Archbishop Raymond G. Hunthausen of Seattle and Auxiliary Bishop Thomas J. Gumbleton of Detroit—discussed the letter on the Phil Donahue television program. (Donahue, an embittered ex-Catholic, has often used his influence to promote the cause of abortion.) The two bishops were offered a golden opportunity, but it was one they declined. Abortion was not mentioned on the program.

Bishop Kenneth Untener of Saginaw, Michigan, is one of three bishops charged with overseeing the dissemination of the pastoral to a wider audience. Shortly after its issuance Bishop Untener stated that it was intended to be an ecumenical document. Almost in the same breath, however, he made a speech severely critical of popular Protestant evangelists, whom he accused of corrupting religion.[16] Clearly he did not seek ecumenical support in that direction; yet it was from that direction that the Catholic bishops have received support for their campaign against abortion. Obviously the new pastoral enabled Bishop Untener to change directions and to make common cause with liberal Protestants, who could accept the pastoral's conclusions about war and peace without accepting its reasoning and, above all, without accepting its statements about abortion. Secularized liberals had no need to regret the abortion clause because they sensed, from the beginning, that it was not of the essence of the document.

This confusion in turn reveals other subterranean aspects of the debate over the pastoral. For example, the journalists Rowland Evans and Robert Novak speculated that the document had been inspired by liberals within the church, including some bishops, who were dismayed at the way in which the abortion issue had led many Catholics to vote for conservative Republican candidates for public office, thus contributing to the election of Ronald Reagan in 1980. According to this scenario, the letter on war and peace was to establish a new moral priority for American Catholics, replacing the priority of abortion. This in turn would justify a return to the Democratic fold by Catholics in 1984.[17]

How much truth lies behind such speculation is impossible to judge. Certainly a majority of the bishops do not regret their commitment to the anti-abortion cause, although the same cannot necessarily be said about their advisors. In practice they have created a seemingly insoluble dilemma for Catholics who sincerely want to be guided by Catholic morality in the voting booth—whether to support a candidate who opposes both legalized abortion and a nuclear freeze, or one who favors both. The practical result is likely to be to weaken the political impact of both the anti-abortion and the antinuclear constituencies, insofar as either can claim religious sanction.

There is no doubt that the issuance of the pastoral letter in 1983 marks the culmination of a kind of revolution in American Catholicism. This is true less in terms of its contents (although it bears distinct traces of that revolution) than in the circumstances surrounding it.

Since the time of the Second Vatican Council, a growing body of clergy and other professionals within the church have been interpreting their religion primarily in terms compatible with the dominant American liberalism. This has meant not only predictable stands on most public issues—war and peace, the welfare state, the Third World— but also a liberal view of the church itself, including a deemphasis on hierarchical authority and dogma in favor of a posture of "searching" and communal exploration. Usually the two go together; those Catholics who wish to revise dogmas and moral laws and make the church more internally democratic tend also to believe that the church proves its relevance to the present age by taking a progressive stand on controversial public issues. Gradually this mentality has taken hold among a significant minority of the bishops themselves. [18]

Much of the impetus for the letter came from a handful of celebrated "peace bishops," who had been pressing the issue for several years and for whom the lopsided approval of the letter was a major victory. Some of their own views are quite extreme, although the final letter reflects those views only obliquely.

Thus Archbishop Hunthausen has said that the United States should surrender to an invader rather than offer armed resistance, and he has been refusing to pay parts of his income tax because he regards national defense as inherently immoral. [19]

Bishop Walter F. Sullivan of Richmond has denied any significant moral difference between the United States and the Soviet Union, asserting that "I just think that we are as aggressive as Russia as far as using nations for our benefit." On another occasion he argued that the Soviets have been willing to observe a reliable arms-control treaty but the United States has not and that the Soviets cannot trust the United States. [20]

Bishop Maurice F. Dingman of Des Moines, when asked the inevitable question about the Soviet Union, says that he feels impelled to oppose the American arms build-up because of the negative example of the German and Italian bishops of the 1930s—World War II might have been averted if they had opposed the policies of their governments.[21] Obviously, to Dingman, the United States is the present moral equivalent of the Fascist states of the 1930s. Presumably, in this equation, the Soviet Union is merely a passive victim of American aggression.

The bishops in question, along with other leaders among the "peace bishops"—retired Bishop Carroll T. Dozier of Memphis, Bishop Gumbleton, and Archbishop Peter L. Gerety of Newark—have consistently supported persons and causes at odds with official Catholic teaching on other questions. In them there has been a coming together of the two strands of the "new church."[22]

For some within the church the process by which the pastoral was formed was at least as important as its contents. It was intended not to be prophetic, if by prophetic is meant an authoritative pronouncement by a sage who dares to go against accepted opinion. Instead the letter was to be the orchestration of as broad a consensus as possible, inside and outside the church, a process on which the bishops would place their formal stamp of approval. It was intended to serve as a model for other such exercises (future letters are planned on economics and on women), the ultimate result of which will be that bishops are no longer regarded as authoritative teachers but as "facilitators" of community opinion. For many of their newly found admirers what the bishops said in their letter was less important than what their very issuance of it implied. They had shown themselves susceptible to certain kinds of liberal pressure, and it was assumed that they could be led even farther (and on many different subjects) in the future.

Some commentators, such as Arthur Jones of the leftist *National Catholic Reporter,* saw the forging of the document as a kind of declaration of independence from Rome. The

American bishops were "moving ahead of the Vatican" and assuming for themselves the leadership of the worldwide Catholic church. Their experience in doing so would serve them in good stead when they approached other controversial issues, such as the ordination of women to the priesthood.[23] (There was considerable chagrin at the *Reporter* when the Vatican reclaimed a large measure of control over the process.)[24] Later Bishop Gumbleton told a European audience that "We don't expect the Vatican to approve or disapprove of our letter. We take full responsibility for its contents."[25] So also the passage of the letter was a signal to some in the secular community that a different kind of bishop was now in control of the Catholic church in the United States.

On one level this was blatantly political. The Reagan administration handled the matter rather ineptly, first seeming to pressure the bishops into trimming their moral sails, then claiming to have succeeded, which predictably caused leading bishops to emphasize their differences with the administration.[26] But even apart from the mistakes of the White House itself, prominent liberal journalists were gleeful that the bishops seemed to be in confrontation with the government.[27] (This tension served the liberal bishops well, since they could enjoy the plaudits of much of the secular world while still claiming the prophet's mantle because they were in conflict with the incumbent administration.)

As Evans and Novak speculated, some of this had to do explicitly with abortion. Senator Edward Kennedy of Massachusetts, who has consistently voted in favor of abortion on the grounds that he does not mix religion and politics, inserted the pastoral letter in the *Congressional Record*.[28] At a conference on the pastoral held in a Catholic church on Capitol Hill, the principal speaker was Senator Patrick Leahy of Vermont, also an unwavering proponent of abortion.[29] Peter Henriot, a prominent leftist Jesuit in Washington, was quick to point out that the letter had provoked a confrontation with a president who supported two key Catholic issues—restricting abortions and granting public aid to private schools.[30] Although the leaders among the bishops insisted that the document was "nonpolitical," in practice there was no way it could have avoided being political, a point some of its strongest supporters understood quite well.

In this regard one of the most curious of the circumstances surrounding the document was the symbiotic relationship which was established between some bishops and elements in the liberal media hitherto not inclined to be friendly. For example, Evarts Graham of the St. Louis *Post-Dispatch* condescendingly praised the bishops for having risen above the limitations of their immigrant background.[31] Marjorie Hyer of the Washington *Post,* who had once gleefully reported that "audible groans swept over the house" of bishops whenever one of its more conservative members rose to speak, also saw the war/peace letter as marking a kind of "maturing" of the American church.[32]

Most candid was Mary McGrory, also of the Washington *Post.* She too was gleeful over the bishops' "veering off into a cosmic 'prolife' movement" which flew in the face of the Reagan administration's anti-abortion stance, and she chuckled over bishops who "have grown hoarse preaching against the godless Soviet system" suddenly shifting their position. Once allegedly interested only in sexual morality and bingo, these bishops had "grown up," as evidenced in their new concern for "important" issues.[33]

Some of the bishops seemed to welcome this demeaning

praise, and to interpret their role in the same terms. The president of the American hierarchy, Archbishop John R. Roach of St. Paul-Minneapolis, said, for example, that the letter marked the "coming of age of a more robust church" and a church which finds itself "comfortable with a very public posture on a very public issue."[34] It was a remark which made sense only if the bishops' previous prominent role in the anti-abortion movement was discounted.

Mary McGrory's analysis also made explicit what remained unstated by other commentators—that by turning their attentions to the war/peace issue the bishops were turning away from a now outmoded concern for the things of heaven. A bishop who suggested that sin is a graver evil than nuclear destruction and said, "Our striving is not for survival but for resurrection," was a "lone voice," she noted.[35]

If the letter of the bishops' text is adhered to strictly, it can perhaps be said that they ended by issuing a reasonably balanced document. But the trouble lies there—if the letter were as "moderate" as it appears, it would not be the subject of such enthusiastic encomia from people who ordinarily show scant respect for Catholic bishops. The letter has been regarded as important less for what it says explicitly than for what it seems to portend about the future of the Catholic church in the United States.

Numerous liberal commentators have noted with delight that the bishops seem to be "getting over" their traditional anticommunism. (What they said about Soviet Russia explicitly can be overlooked as a mere atavism.) They are moving away from their earlier uncompromising stand on abortion. (This too can be dismissed as merely a piece of baggage the bishops cannot quickly discard.) Perhaps most important, they seem at last to be shedding the distinctive way Catholics have of viewing the world and are coming to see it in the same way it is viewed in the liberal media. In a real sense the bishops seem to desire liberal media approval in ways they never did before.

During the debates, Archbishop Oscar Lipscomb of Mobile reminded his fellow prelates that "We speak of preservation of the planet as almost an absolute. We seem to be seeking the eternal life of the human species—which is not at the heart of biblical teaching."[36] It was a telling point, because all the misgivings about the entire pastoral enterprise could be subsumed under the single great misgiving as to why this particular subject was chosen at this particular time, and was addressed in this particular way.

When Catholic bishops addressed themselves to the subject of war and peace in earlier years, they acted with a strong sense that man is under divine judgment because of sin and that true peace will be attained only when sinful human beings repent and turn again to obey God's laws.[37] The 1983 pastoral contains little of this idea. Undoubtedly an approach to peace which rooted it in the fundamental relationship between man and God would be incomprehensible to many who look for "prophecy" from the bishops. It is possible to agree substantially with the contents of the pastoral and still regard it as a radically incomplete document. It is also possible to agree with it substantially while harboring grave misgivings as to why the bishops chose to take up this subject at the moment in history when it has become a fashionable secular cause, and why they have chosen to address it in terms which fashionable secularists find acceptable. As Archbishop Lipscomb's intervention suggested, in choosing the nuclear-weapons issue as their chief priority, the bishops seem to have shifted their perspective drastically from the things of eternity to the things of this world.

Such an analysis was at least half-wishful, a reflection as much of the religious obtuseness of the media as of the reality being described. The great majority of the American bishops are devout, orthodox Catholics. However, among their number are a few who see the world in terms not essentially different from those of the Washington *Post*. Even more troubling, the entire process by which the war/peace letter was drafted and issued was from the beginning orchestrated toward that purpose. It was a morality play in which "bad" conservative Catholics were seen as being vanquished by "good" liberal Catholics, much of the action precisely a shift of emphasis from "irrelevant" religious considerations to "important" political ones. Even as the formula for social relevance had been revealed as bankrupt in liberal Protestantism, it was being adopted by some Catholic bishops.

Those Christians most anxious to show themselves "prophetic" are perhaps among those least likely to be so. The governing irony of the American bishops is the fact that many of them are irresolute and confused with regard to internal church matters where Catholic doctrine is clear and consistent. They find it impossible to take a firm stand on questions such as divorce, homosexuality, the demand of women to be ordained to the priesthood, and priestly celibacy. Often they fail to exert discipline or leadership when either church law or doctrine is being flouted. It is almost as though, having found it impossible to govern the church as they should, they have decided to try instead to govern the nation.

Such a jibe is, however, unfair, because the issues of war and peace are supremely important. If religious leaders cannot take a stand on such questions, there are very few on which they are qualified to speak. What remains for the Catholic bishops is not to take back those of their words which may have given offense but to resolve to manifest to the world their ability to intervene in a timely public debate and their ability to recall a floundering world to the Source of its life, where alone it can find the peace it seeks.

---

1. The complete text is in *Origins* (Washington: National Catholic News Service), May 19, 1983.

2. *Catholic Mind,* Mar. 1982, pp. 31–36.

3. *Origins,* Oct. 28, 1982.

4. *Origins,* Apr. 14, 1983.

5. For a sampling of the debate, from various points of view, see *National Catholic Register,* Dec. 26, 1982, pp. 1, 8, 10; *Catholicism in Crisis,* Dec 982; Jan., Feb. 1983; *Fellowship of Catholic Scholars Newsletter,* Sept., Dec. 1982; Mar. 1983; *National Catholic Reporter,* Nov. 5, 1982; and *The Wanderer,* May 19, 1983, pp. 1, 6.

6. See, for example, Curran, et al., *Dissent in and for the Church* (New York: Herder and Herder, 1969).

7. See especially the discussions in the *Fellowship of Catholic Scholars Newsletter,* as in note 5 above.

8. See the critique of Rev. William B. Smith in the *National Catholic Register,* May 8, 1983, p. 5.

9. For example, John Paul II reminded the United Nations that: "In the course of the last ten years your organizations have too often been the object of attempts at manipulation on the part of nations wishing to exploit such bodies." He went on to call on them to undergo "qualitative change" and "even to reform on certain points . . ." (quoted in the final draft of the pastoral letter, p. 11).

10 For accounts of the Vatican meeting see the *National Catholic Reporter,* Jan. 28, 1983, pp. 1, 18, and Apr. 29, 1983, pp. 1, 20, 23; *The Wanderer,* Apr. 28, 1983, p. 7· and St. Louis *Post-Dispatch,* Jan. 18, 1983, p. 8A.

11. As reported in the *National Catholic Reporter,* May 13, 1983, pp. 1, 21; and *The Wanderer,* May 12, 1983, pp. 1, 6.

12. Quoted in the St. Louis *Review,* Apr. 1, 1983, p. 2.

13. Reported in the *National Catholic Reporter,* May 6, 1983, p. 3.

14. See, for example, the criticism of Jim Wallis, *Sojourners,* Apr. 1983; Wallis and Gene Laroque, as quoted in the St. Louis *Post-Dispatch,* Mar. 20, 1983, p. 3E; Garry Wills, as quoted in the St. Louis *Review,* Apr. 29, 1983, p. 11; and Colman McCarthy, Washington *Post,* Nov. 14, 1982.

15. See, for example, St. Louis *Review,* Nov. 12, 1982, p. 1; May 20, 1983, p. 2; May 27, 1983, p. 1; St. Louis *Post-Dispatch,* May 8, 1983, p. 6A; May 14, 1983, p. 9A; New York *Times,* May 30, 1983, pp. 21, 24.

16. Quoted in the *National Catholic Register,* May 29, 1983, p. 2.

17. Reprinted in *The Wanderer,* May 12, 1983, p. 4.

18. For a discussion of this phenomenon, see J. Brian Benestad, *The Pursuit of a Just Social Order* (Washington: Ethics and Public Policy Center, 1983) and Joseph A. Varacalli, *Towards the Establishment of Liberal Catholicism in America* (Washington: University Press of America, 1982).

19. Quoted in *The Wanderer,* Nov. 25, 1982, p. 4.

20. Quoted in the St. Louis *Review,* Oct. 15, 1982, p. 6; and in the Washington *Post,* June 5, 1983, p. C5.

21. Quoted by John McCormally in the Hays, Kansas, *Daily News,* Dec. 3, 1982, p. 4A, and May 8, 1983, p. 4. See also Bishop Dingman's remarks in the New York *Times,* May 8, 1983, p. E5.

22. See Hitchcock, *The Dissenting Church* (New York: National Committee of Catholic Laymen, 1983).

23. *National Catholic Reporter,* Jan. 28, 1983, p. 24, and Feb. 4, 1983, p. 24.

24. Ibid., Apr. 29, 1983, pp. 1, 20, 23. At one point the *Reporter* claimed (Feb. 11, 1983, pp. 1, 26) that the Vatican had given the bishops approval to go "beyond" its own position, a claim which was formally denied by the bishops' official spokesman (St. Louis *Review,* Feb. 18, 1983, pp. 1, 7).

25. Quoted in the *National Catholic Reporter,* May 27, 1983, p. 26.

26. Ibid., Apr. 15, 1983, p. 5.

27. See, for example, the comments of Mary McGrory in the St. Louis *Post-Dispatch,* Nov. 19, 1982, p. 15A, and May 11, 1983, p. 17A, and in the Washington *Post,* Apr. 7, 1983, p. A3; those of Marjorie Hyer in the Washington *Post,* Nov. 2, 1982, p. C3; and those of Arthur Jones in the *National Catholic Reporter,* May 13, 1983, p. 24.

28. May 16, 1983, pp. S6669 *et seq.*
29. See the account in *The Wanderer*, May 19, 1983, pp. 1, 6.
30. Quoted in the St. Louis *Post-Dispatch*, May 6, 1983, p. 9D.
31. Ibid., Nov. 24, 1982, p. 21A.
32. Washington *Post*, Nov. 21, 1980, p. F10, and Nov. 2, 1982, p. A3.
33. Ibid., Nov. 21, 1982, pp. C1, 5.
34. Quoted in the St. Louis *Post-Dispatch*, Nov. 19, 1982, p. 1A.
35. Washington *Post*, Nov. 21, 1982, pp. C1, 5.
36. Quoted in the St. Louis *Post-Dispatch*, Nov. 19, 1982, p. 12A.
37. See, for example, Hugh J. Nolan (ed.), *Pastoral Letters of the American Hierarchy, 1792-1970* (Huntington, Ind.: Our Sunday Visitor Press, 1971), pp. 335–7, 372–409, 481–6, 493–6, 515–20.